THE HYMNS OF ŚANKARA

THE HYMNS OF ŚAṄKARA

T. M. P. MAHADEVAN

MOTILAL BANARSIDASS
Delhi Varanasi Patna Madras

First Edition Delhi 1980, Reprint 1986

MOTILAL BANARSIDASS
Bungalow Road, Jawahar Nagar, Delhi 110 007
Branches
Chowk, Varanasi 221 001
Ashok Rajpath, Patna 800 004
6 Appar Swamy Koil Street, Mylapore, Madras 600 004

ISBN : 81–208–0094–X (Cloth)
ISBN : 81–208–0097–4 (Paper)

PRINTED IN INDIA
BY JAINENDRA PRAKASH JAIN AT SHRI JAINENDRA PRESS, A-45 NARAINA INDUSTRIAL AREA, PHASE I, NEW DELHI 110 028 AND PUBLISHED BY NARENDRA PRAKASH JAIN FOR MOTILAL BANARSIDASS, DELHI 110 007

TO

THE JAGADGURU
Who is the Sixty-eighth
in the hallowed line of succession
from Śrī Śaṅkara Bhagavatpāda
in the Śrī Kāñcī Kāmakoti Piṭha
as the Presiding Preceptor
with deep devotion, respectful regards,
and reverential salutations

अस्माकं यद्द्विदाज्ञानमज्ञानेन प्रवर्धितम् ।
तन्नाशनं कुरु गुरो ! मोक्षदो भव सन्ततम् ।।

O, Preceptor! Do Thou remove our knowledge of duality nurtured by ignorance; and be Thou at all times the one who grants us liberation.

Plate 1

Śrī Śaṅkara (Facing Preface)

PREFACE TO THE FIRST EDITION

In connection with Śrī Śaṅkara Jayanti celebrations at Śaṅkara Vihar, Ayanavaram, every year I have been privileged to bring out a small publication based on the works either of Śrī Śaṅkara or about Him under the head 'Jayanti Series'. The first book in the Series, *A Morning Prayer and Hymn to Dakṣiṇāmūrti*, was published in 1956. Then followed *Īśāvāsya Upaniṣad* (No. 2, 1957), *Kena Upaniṣad* (No. 3, 1958), *Homage to Śaṅkara* (No. 4, 1959), *Readings from Śaṅkara* (Part One, No. 5, 1960), *Readings from Śaṅkara* (Part Two, No. 6, 1961), *Bhaja Govindam* (No. 7, 1962), *Hymn to Śiva* (No. 8. 1963), *Self-knowledge* (No. 9, 1964), *Vedānta in ten Verses* (No. 10, 1965), and *The Wisdom of Unity* (No. 11, 1967). As some of these publications have gone out of print, they are being reprinted here either in full or in part. The present publication, *The Hymns of Śaṅkara* is No. 12 in the Series. Among its contents, the *Hymn to Dakṣiṇāmūrti* is taken from No. 1 in the Series, the *Hymn to Guru* from No. 4, the *Bhaja Govindam* from No. 7, and the *Śivānandalaharī* is a reproduction of No. 8. There are two appendices. One is *Mānasollāsa* taken from No. 1 in the Series and the other is *Toṭakāṣṭaka* taken from No. 4. I thank Messrs. Ganesh and Co., for sponsoring the publication of this number. I am grateful to Dr N. Veezhinathan for reading the proofs.

Madras
April 20, 1970

T. M. P. Mahadevan

PREFACE TO THE REVISED EDITION

The "Hymns of Śaṅkara" first published in 1970 has long been out of print. I am happy that the present Revised Edition is being sponsored by the well known Indological publishers Messrs Motilal Banarsidass.

I am grateful to Sri N. P. Jain for agreeing immediately and unhesitatingly to accept my proposal to bring out this Revised Edition.

The version of my commentary on the "Hymn to Dakṣiṇāmūrti" is entirely a new one based on Svayamprakāśa-yati's *vyākhyāna*.

Madras
May 1, 1980

T. M. P. Mahadevan

CONTENTS

ILLUSTRATIONS

Śrī Śaṅkara (Facing Preface)
Śrī Dakṣiṇāmurti (Facing P. 1)
Śrī Govinda (Facing P. 33)
Śrī Śaṅkara with four disciples (Facing P. 173)

Plate 2

Śrī Dakṣiṇāmūrti

(Facing p. 1)

I

HYMN TO DAKṢIṆĀMŪRTI*

The Hymn to Dakṣiṇāmūrti has rightly become famous. In a short compass it gives the quintessence of Advaita. It is addressed to God as, *Guru*, by whose grace one receives the teaching of non-duality. How the one reality appears as the many, how even the distinction of the teacher and the taught comes about one cannot explain. But the basic truth of Advaita, which is the Self, of the nature of consciousness, cannot be denied. Whether it is called God, *Guru*, or Self, it is the same. The realization of this truth is the goal of Advaita. And, Advaita is in opposition to no school of thought or mode of spiritual life. In order to show this, Śaṅkara employs in this Hymn some of the terms peculiar to Kashmir Śaivism.

मौनव्याख्याप्रकटितपरब्रह्मतत्त्वं युवानं
वर्षिष्ठान्तेवसदृषिगणैरावृतं ब्रह्मनिष्ठैः ।
आचार्येन्द्रं करकलितचिन्मुद्रमानन्दमूर्तिं
स्वात्मारामं मुदितवदनं दक्षिणामूर्तिमीडे ॥

maunavyākhyā-prakaṭitaparabrahmatattvaṁ yuvānaṁ
varṣiṣṭhāntevasadṛṣigaṇairāvṛtaṁ brahmaniṣṭhaiḥ/
ācāryendraṁ karakalita-cinmudram-ānandamūrtiṁ
svātmārāmaṁ muditavadanaṁ dakṣiṇāmūrtimīḍe//

---

*The explanation is based on Svayamprakāśa-yati's commentary, *Tattvasudhā*.

I praise Dakṣiṇāmūrti, the handsome youth who has expounded the truth of non-duality by eloquent silence, who is surrounded by a group of disciples consisting of aged sages who are absorbed in the contemplation of the supreme Self, who is the prince among preceptors, who by his hand (i.e., by the union of his thumb and the fore-finger) shows the sign indicating the identity of the individual soul and the supreme Self, who is the embodiment of bliss, who delights in the Self, and who has a charming face.

1

विश्वं दर्पणदृश्यमाननगरीतुल्यं निजान्तर्गतं
पश्यन्नात्मनि मायया बहिरिवोद्भूतं यथा निद्रया ।
यः साक्षात्कुरुते प्रबोधसमये स्वात्मानमेवाद्वयं
तस्मै श्रीगुरुमूर्तये नम इदं श्रीदक्षिणामूर्तये ॥

viśvaṁ darpaṇa-dṛśyamāna-nagarī-tulyaṁ nijāntargataṁ
paśyann-ātmani māyayā bahirivodbhūtaṁ yathā nidrayā/
yaḥ sākṣātkurute prabodha-samaye svātmānamevādvayaṁ
tasmai śrī-gurumūrtaye nama idaṁ śrī-dakṣiṇāmūrtaye//

To Him who by *māyā* as by dream, sees within Himself the universe which is inside Him, like unto a city that is seen in a mirror, (but) which is manifested as if without : to Him who apprehends, at the time of awakening, His own non-dual Self : to Him, of the form of the Preceptor, the blessed Dakṣiṇāmūrti may this obeisance be !

In this well-known hymn addressed to the Supreme Divinity appearing as Preceptor, Śrī Śaṅkara expounds the Truth of Advaita.

One of the forms in which Lord Śiva is pictured is that of the youthful world-teacher seated beneath the sacred fig-tree, facing South, and teaching elderly disciples through silence. The significance of this form is the supreme identity of God (*Īśvara*), Teacher (*Guru*), and Self (*Ātman*). It is the same Self that appears as God and as the soul, as the teacher and as the taught.

The commentator, Svayaṁprakāśa-yati, introduces the *Hymn* thus :

The Bhāṣyakāra (i.e. Śaṅkara), the omniscient Lord, embodied himself forth, with the sole aim of bestowing grace unto the world. In order to fulfil this aim, he exhibited through enquiry into the Vedāntic texts, with the help of reasoning, that Advaita is the supreme purport. The Vedāntic texts may be compared to the Milk-Ocean, reasoning to the Mandara hill which was used as the churning rod, the process of enquiry to the churning, and Advaita to the ambrosia that emerged from the Milk-Ocean. Collecting the ambrosia, Śaṅkara has kept it in the present hymn which serves as the vessel to preserve it for distribution.

The essence of the teaching that is thus preserved is that the so-called individual soul (*jīva*) that is the enjoyer, the universe which is the object enjoyed, the supreme Lord who is the giver of enjoyment and the *Guru* who grants release, are absolutely non-different (i.e. one). By a devoted study of this hymn, by reflecting on its teaching, and by meditating on the truth taught, one will gain the supreme end which is release.

The hymn has already been compared to the vessel that serves as a receptacle for the ambrosia (i.e. Advaita). It may also be likened unto the butter that is churned out of the milk of Vedānta.

In the first verse, it is shown that the South-facing Śiva, the supreme Lord who is the Self, is the substrate of the entire universe. The manifold universe consisting of the elements and the elementals exists in one's Self. The Self is one; the world is manifold. The Self is unchanging; the world is subject of ceaseless-change. The Self is infinite; the world consists of finite entities. The Self is pure; the world is full of impurities. How can the former be the substrate of the latter? This is explained with the help of an example. The world appears in the Self like the city with its streets and buildings, market-places and business-houses, tanks and towers, vehicles and living beings in a clear, unsoiled mirror. The mirrored city is not real; and yet it appears in the mirror.

It may be asked : If the world remains always in the Self, it must be experienced like desire, anger, etc., inside of us and not outside. To this, it is replied : *Māyā* (which is the same as *avidyā* or *ajñāna*) has the self-luminous Self as its locus (*āśraya*) and content (*viṣaya*); just as in bright sun-light the owl sees darkness, in the self-luminous Self there is *māyā* veiling it. The evidence for this is the experience "I do not know myself." From this it is clear that the Self is locus as well as content of ignorance.

An example for the appearance, outside, of what is within is dream-experience. The dream-world is what is superimposed on the Self which is the witness; yet it appears as if outside the Self. Similarly in the state of waking, one sees the world which is superimposed on one's Self, as if it exists outside. Because of the superimposition of identity with the body, etc., which are superimposed on the Self, one sees the world as if it exists outside. No relation of the world which is inert, such as conjunction and inherence, is possible with the Self which is consciousness. If it were not for superimposition on the self-luminous Self, the world would not even be manifest. Therefore, the world is only a superimposition on the Self.

Objection : If it is true that the world is what is superimposed on the Self, it should be sublated. But we do not experience its sublation at any time. Therefore, the world is not what is superimposed on the Self; it exists really outside the Self.

Reply : Just as the dream-world, even though super-imposed, shines at the time of dreaming as if it is real, but is sublated when one wakes up, even so, this waking world too, although it is manifest as if real before the rise of true knowledge, gets sublated, along with its cause which is nescience, at the time when there arises the knowledge of identity of the inner Self and *Brahman* through the major texts such as *That thou art*, as taught by the supremely compassionate and gracious *Ācārya* who is an incarnation of *Parameśvara* (the supreme Lord). When there is the direct experience (*sākṣātkāra*) of this truth, what remains unsublated is only the non-dual *Brahman* which is the Self.

The non-dual *Brahman* is free from limitations caused by space, time, and other things. The direct experience of *Brahman* is gained through the grace of the Guru who is God.

parādvaitasya vijñānaṁ kṛpayā vai dadāti yaḥ|
so'yaṁ gurur-gurus-sākṣāt śiva eva na saṁśayaḥ||

"He who grants, out of compassion, the knowledge of the supreme Non-duality is, verily, the *Guru* who is Śiva Himself. There is no doubt in regard to this".

Śrī Dakṣiṇāmūrti is the *Ādi Guru*. The term means 'the auspicious form of Śiva that faces the southern direction' (*dakṣiṇa-dig-abhimukhā mūrtiḥ*). It may also be interpreted to mean : 'He who is expert (*dakṣiṇaḥ*) in accomplishing the origination, sustentation, and destruction of the world, through His beginningless and wonderful power of *māyā* (*śrī*), and yet is, in truth, without form (*amūrta*).

śriyā dakṣiṇaḥ śrī-dakṣiṇaḥ; sa ca asau amūrtiśca|

Offering obeisance, in the present context, means 'surrendering oneself to the supreme Lord, in oneness' (*prahvībhāvaḥ svātmanaḥ parameśvare ekatvena samarpaṇam*). It is the realisation of the non-difference of the implied meanings of 'that' and 'thou'. The express sense of 'that' is *Īśvara* (God); the express sense of 'thou' is *jīva* (soul); the implied meaning of both the words is the Self which is pure consciousness.

2

बीजस्यान्तरिवाङ्कुरो जगदिदं प्राङ्निर्विकल्पं पुन-
र्मायाकल्पितदेशकालकलनावैचित्र्यचित्रीकृतम् ।
मायावीव विजृम्भयत्यपि महायोगीव यः स्वेच्छया
तस्मै श्रीगुरुमूर्तये नम इदं श्रीदक्षिणामूर्तये ॥

bījasyāntarivāṅkuro jagad idaṁ prāṅ-nirvikalpaṁ punar-
māyā-kalpita-deśa-kāla-kalanā-vaicitrya-citrīkṛtam|
māyāvīva vijṛmbhayaty api mahāyogīva yaḥ svecchayā
tasmai śrī-gurumūrtaye nama idaṁ śrī-dakṣiṇāmūrtaye||

To him who, like a magician or even like a great *Yogin*, displays, by His own will, this universe which at the beginning is undifferentiated like the sprout in the seed, but which is made again differentiated under the varied conditions of space and time posited by *māyā* : to Him, of the form of the Preceptor, the blessed Dakṣiṇāmūrti may this obeisance be !

One of the persistent problems of philosophy and religion is about the causality of the universe. Is there a cause for the world or not? Is the world-cause some blind force, or an intelligent principle? Is that cause one or many ? The different schools of thought give different answers, *Yadṛcchāvāda* (accidentalism) contends that there is no need for a cause of the world; for, according to it, whatever order there is in the world is due to mere chance. *Svabhāvavāda* (naturalism) recognises the law of causation, but holds that the world is self-caused. *Cārvāka* (materialism) traces all things to the four elements, earth, water, fire and air. Nyāya-Vaiśeṣika believes that the constituents of the natural world are composed of material atoms, and that the Prime Mover of these atoms is God. The Sāṅkhya finds no use for a God, invests Primal Matter (*Prakṛti*) with perpetual movement, and regards the presence of the sentient soul (*Puruṣa*) only as the occasioning cause for evolution to start. Some schools of Vedānta think that God is the efficient cause of the universe, and that *Prakṛti* is the material cause. Some others maintain that God is the sole and whole cause of the world, and that the world is a real transformation (*pariṇāma*) of a part of Him.

Advaita Vedānta is not satisfied with any of the above mentioned views. The variegated and intelligently ordered universe cannot be the result of chance. Even to say that it is the *result* of chance is to accept causation. The world cannot be self-caused, because the world itself is inert, and one and the same thing cannot be both the agent and the patient of a process. Neither the elements nor the atoms, nor *Prakṛti* can account for the universe; for they are all non-intelligent. God cannot be merely the efficient cause, for, if He were to shape the universe out of some stuff which is external to Him, He would become conditioned thereby. Nor can the universe be considered a transformation of God; for a God that changes cannot be immutable. So, Advaita concludes that the universe is an illusory appearance (*vivarta*) of the absolute spirit. The world is a play of *māyā* (*māyā-vilāsa*). That is why Śaṅkara, in the present verse, compares God to the magician and the *Yogin*. In the illusions created by these, nothing really happens. It is this truth that Guru Dakṣiṇāmūrti teaches.

Now, we shall turn to Svayaṁprakāśa-yati's commentary.

In the first verse, it was stated that the Self is the locus of the world. The objector says that this is impossible. The Self cannot be the cause of the world. If the Self be the cause, is it the originating cause (*ārambhaka*), or is it the transforming cause (*pariṇāmī*) ? The first alternative is not possible. The one, non-dual, all-pervading consciousness cannot be the originating cause of the world which is inert. And so, the Nyāya-Vaiśeṣika view holds that the four types of primary atoms which are eternal are the originating causes of the world. The second alternative that the Self is the transforming cause is also not intelligible. According to the Sāṅkhya, *Prakṛti* or *Pradhāna* (Primal Nature) which consists of three *guṇa-s* (*sattva*, *rajas*, and *tamas*) is the transforming cause of the world. It is in *Prakṛti* that the world truly exists in an unmanifest state prior to evolution, and not in the Self which is pure consciousness.

We shall examine these two views in sequence.

The Nyāya-Vaiśeṣika view that the world is originated from primal atoms does not stand to reason.

(1) The prima latoms, according to the Nyāya-Vaiśeṣika, are partless (*niravayava*). By combining—whatever be their number—they cannot produce anything with magnitude. That which is generated by the atoms in conjunction can only be atomic.

(2) It is maintained that cause and effect are totally different from each other. This is unintelligible. How can two things, entirely different from each other, like cow and horse, be related as cause and effect ?

(3) The Nyāya-Vaiśeṣika theory of causation is *asatkārya-vāda*. The effect is non-existent in the cause prior to its production; it is produced *de novo*. How is this possible ? How can the non-existent, like hare's horn, be produced at all ?

(4) If the effect that is originated is totally different from the cause, then there is the contingence of qualities appearing in it which are radically different. When red threads are woven, blue cloth may emerge. But, this is not what the Nyāya-Vaiśeṣika would endorse. According to this school, the quality that appears in the effect is similar to the quality that is in the cause.

(5) There is no evidence for the existence of what are called primal atoms. The arguments that are advanced are not valid. There is no necessity that the process of dividing a finite thing should have a limit and that that limit should be the partless atom. Granting that the atoms are partless, they cannot combine and constitute wholes consisting of parts. There is no scriptural authority validating the atomic theory.

(6) It is held that effects are produced from causes which are less in size than they. But this is not the case. For instance, threads which are small in size are produced from a cotton-mass which is larger in size.

Thus, the Nyāya-Vaiśeṣika view that the world is originated from primal atoms is not sound.

The Sāṅkhya system maintains that the world is a transformation of *Pradhāna* (*pradhāna-pariṇāma-vāda*). This view, also, is unacceptable. *Pradhāna or Prakṛti* is inert (*jaḍa*). If it is not founded on, or directed by, a principle which is intelligent, it cannot evolve into the world. A chariot, for instance, cannot, of itself, come out of wood. In order for it to be made, there is required an intelligent carpenter.

What are cited by the Sāṅkhya as proofs for the existence of *Pradhāna* are no proofs at all. A passage in the *Śvetāśvatara-upaniṣad* (iv, 5) is quoted in support of the doctrine of *Pradhāna*. The passage refers to the "One Unborn, red, white and black, producing manifold offspring similar in form (to herself)." But, here, the reference is to *māyā*, or *prakṛti*, from which fire, water, earth, etc., are made manifest, and not to the *Pradhāna* of the

Sāṅkhya. Moreover, there are numerous scriptural texts which proclaim that the source of the world is the supreme Self.

The Self is the cause of the illusory appearance (*vivarta*) of the world, even as the rope is the cause of the snake-appearance, and nacre, of the silver-appearance. Just as the dream-world is imagined in the Self, so is the waking world. It is an exercise in error to look for the source of the world, other than the Self. In empirical usage such as the 'pot *exists*,' the cloth '*exists*,' 'the pot is *manifest*,' 'the cloth is *manifest*,' we note that *existence* and *manifestation* are constant in things that vary. It is the Self which is existence-consciousness that is the underlying ground of the world. It is the *whole* and the *sole* cause—the cause of the origination, sustentation, and dissolution of the world.

Before the world was made manifest, it was undifferentiated in its cause, the Self, like the sprout in the seed. *Māyā*, as grounded in *Īśvara*, posits conditions such as space and time, and produces the variegated world, with beings bearing specific names and forms.

Objection: How can *Īśvara*, who is devoid of any external aids, be the generator of the world ? The potter, for instance, can produce a pot only when there are ancillaries such as the wheel, the rod for rotating, etc.

Reply: *Īśvara* has as his adjunct the beginningless, indeterminable *māyā*. With this as his power, and through his mere will, he projects the world, like the magician who weaves an illusion by waving his wand, or like the yogin who can create a new region through his power of *yoga*.

Objection: If there is *māyā* besides *Īśvara* (or the Self), will there not result duality? And, if He is the cause of the world, will He not be subject to modification?

Reply: No. *Māyā* is not real; it is illusory, as the world is. Only if it were a reality besides *Īśvara*, there would be duality. The causality of the world which appears in *Īśvara* is structured by the beginningless, indeterminable *māyā*; and so, the causality also is illusory. No defect whatever is imported into the Self by this causality. It remains blemishless, while being the cause of the origination, sustentation, and dissolution of the world.

3

यस्यैव स्फुरणं सदात्मकमसत्कल्पार्थकं भासते
साक्षात्तत्त्वमसीति वेदवचसा यो बोधयत्याश्रितान् ।
यत्साक्षात्करणाद्भवेन्न पुनरावृत्तिर्भवाम्भोनिधौ
तस्मै श्रीगुरुमूर्तये नम इदं श्रीदक्षिणामूर्तये ॥

yasyaiva sphuraṇaṁ sadātmakam asat-kalpārthakaṁ bhāsate
sākṣāt tattvamasīti veda-vacasā yo bodhayatẏ āśritān|
yat sākṣātkaraṇād bhaven na punarāvṛttir bhavāṁbhonidhau
tasmai śrī-gurumūrtaye nama idaṁ śrī-dakṣiṇāmūrtaye||

To Him whose luminosity alone, which is of the nature of Existence, shines forth entering the objective world which is like unto the non-existent: to Him who instructs those who resort to him through the Vedic text 'That thou art': to Him by realising whom there will be no more return to the ocean of transmigration: to Him, of the form of the Preceptor, the blessed Dakṣiṇāmūrti, may this obeisance be !

Objection: Why should the cause of the world be an existent like *Īśvara* ? May it not be that the world has come out of non-existence, *asat?* It is observed that pot, etc., are originated from the destruction of the lump of clay, etc. When one wakes up from sleep, the phenomena that are seen at the commencement of the waking state are observed to have non-existence as their antecedent. It may, therefore, be inferred that the world as a whole is generated from non-existence. There is also the authority of the Upaniṣadic text which declares, "Non-existent, verily, this was in the beginning."

Reply: Were non-existence the cause of the world, non-existence would be pervasively experienced in the form "pot is non-existent; cloth is non-existent", etc. But, what is pervasively experienced is existence, as "pot exists; cloth exists." Moreover, since non-existence is of the nature of non-manifestation, the world which is said to be from non-existence would also be non-manifest. But, this is contrary to what we experience. We experience the world as existent and as manifest. But the world has no existence of its own, nor manifestation. It is by the existence of its substrate, the Self, that it exists; and it is by the light that is the Self, that it shines, as superimposed on the Self.

It was stated in the objection that the destruction of the lump of clay is the cause of the production of pot. But this is not so. It is the clay that persists in the pot that is its cause. As for the phenomena that appear at the commencement of the waking state, it is not possible that they appear out of nothing. For them, the cause is the Self that is in the state of deep sleep, and which is existence. That in deep sleep there is the Self, we shall establish later on. As for the Upaniṣadic text "Non-existent, verily, this was in the beginning," its meaning is not that non-existence is the cause, but that before origination the world was unmanifest, that it was of the nature of its cause which is pure existence. The view of non-existence being the cause is refuted by the Upaniṣadic text which says: "How can the existent come out of non-existence ?"

It is the Self which is pure existence (*sat*) that is the substrate of the world-appearance. The world has no reality of its own; it is non-real, it is like unto the unreal. The world is not unreal like the sky-flower or the horns of a hare; nor is it real which the Self alone is. That is why it is said to be indeterminable (*anirvacanīya*). It is what is illusorily superimposed on the substrate Self, like the serpent on the rope or silver on nacre. The world has no reality apart from the Self; nor can it become manifest but for the consciousness which is the Self.

The notion that the non-real world is real, that the not-self (i.e the body, etc.) is the self is the cause of transmigration. Its removal is through the Guru's instruction. The supreme Lord, assuming the form of the Guru, imparts to the disciple the meaning of the *mahāvākya*: *tat tvam asi* (that thou art). The primary meaning of the word 'that' is the omniscient, omnipotent God who is the cause of the universe. The primary meaning of the word 'thou' is the soul endowed with a psycho-physical organism. The two words in the text are put in apposition with each other; and so the text teaches the non-difference of the 'that' and the 'thou'. This, however, would be intelligible only when the adjuncts such as the causality of the universe and limitation by a psycho-physical organism are left out, and the basic pure consciousness alone is understood. Thus the teaching of the *mahā-vākya* is that the Self is all. The Self admits of no relation, such as whole-part, cause-effect, class-individual, substance-attribute, worshipped-worshipper, etc. It is true that without these relations empirical life would be impossible. But empirical life is a matrix of contradictions and seeks fulfilment in its transcendence. The transcendent reality is the pure Self which knows no distinction. It is only when this is realised that there is final freedom from sorrow.

A parallel statement to 'That thou art' is 'This is that Devadatta'. I see a man at present in Cidambaram and recognise him to be the same Devadatta whom I saw last year in Kāśī. The differences in time, place, and other conditions are left out, and the identity of the person 'Devadatta' is asserted in the statement 'This is that Devadatta'. The mode of interpreting the meaning of the statement is known as *bhāga-tyāga-lakṣaṇā or jahad-ajahal-lakṣaṇā* (exclusive-non-exclusive-implication). The 'this' and the 'that' are excluded, and the common part 'Devadatta' is taken as the purport of the statement. Similarly, the *mahā-vākya tat tvam asi* means that the pure consciousness which is the Self is recognised to be the same, one and non-dual, when the limiting adjuncts have been removed.

When the Guru imparts this instruction to the competent pupil, there is instant realisation. The direct knowledge removes the ignorance or nescience which is the cause of transmigration. It is the listening to the *mahā-vākya* that brings about the dawn of knowledge which removes nescience and occasions the release of the soul from bondage.

The objection that, even after the knowledge resulting from the *mahā-vākya*, bondage may continue, as in deep sleep and deluge, is not valid, because while in these states nescience continues, it is destroyed when knowledge arises. For the soul that has realised the truth, there is no more return to the empirical cycle of birth and death. The *Upaniṣads* declare: "The knower of the Self crosses sorrow", "He who knows Brahman is Brahman", "He does not return to *saṁsāra*."

4

नानाच्छिद्र घटोदरस्थितमहादीपप्रभाभास्वरं
ज्ञानं यस्य तु चक्षुरादिकरणद्वारा बहिः स्पन्दते ।
जानामीति तमेव भान्तमनुभात्येतत्समस्तं जगत्
तस्मै श्रीगुरुमूर्तये नम इदं श्रीदक्षिणामूर्तये ॥

nānācchidra-ghaṭodarasthita-mahādīpa-prabhā-bhāsvaraṁ
jñānaṁ yasya tu cakṣurādi-karaṇa-dvārā bahiḥ spandate/
jānāmīti tam-eva bhāntam anubhāty etat samastaṁ jagat
tasmai śrī-gurumūrtaye nama idaṁ śrī-dakṣiṇāmūrtaye//

To Him who is luminous like the light of a great lamp set in the belly of a pot with many holes: to Him whose knowledge moves outward through the eye and other organs: to Him, who shining as 'I know', all this entire universe shines after: to Him of the form of the Preceptor, the blessed Dakṣiṇāmūrti, may this obeisance be!

Objection: Why should we believe that the world's existence and manifestation are derived from the Self which is existence and consciousness? May not the world have independent existence and manifestation, like the Self?

Reply: No; because if the world were independently existent and manifest, like the Self, it should not have origination and destruction; moreover, it should be ever manifest, and also be aware without depending on instruments such as the sense-organs. Since the world has no intrinsic existence and manifestation, it appears and shines because of the Existence-consciousness which is the Self.

Objection: If the entire world is what is superimposed on the Self and shines by its light, why should there be dependence on instruments such as the sense-organs? By the mere relation to the Self which is of the nature of consciousness, why should not everything, always, shine? If it be said that the world does not shine because it is veiled by ignorance (*ajñāna*) which is not opposed to the all-pervading consciousness, then why should the world shine sometimes ? If it be said that the world shines when ignorance is removed, how does the removal of ignorance take place? Since ignorance cannot be removed by anything other than consciousness which is the Self, and since the Self, according to you, is not opposed to ignorance, the world should be ever shrouded in darkness.

In the present verse, the Master gives the answer.

The source of light, both for the individual and the cosmos, is the Self. The individual is able to know objects because of the luminosity of the Self. The objective universe can be known because of the light of the Self. In self-consciousness, of the form 'I know', it is the Self that is Awareness. But for the basic Awareness, none can know and nothing can be known. It is true that this awareness is not evident at first. That is because it is hidden in *avidyā*, nescience, even as a lamp placed within a pot remains unseen. But it is not a hermetically sealed pot that contains the lamp; it has several holes through which the light of the lamp streams forth. Similarly, *avidyā* is itself made manifest by the Self. There are many chinks in it which give it away. In the body-mind complex which is a product of *avidyā*, for instance, there are avenues of knowledge. The sense-organs are not themselves the sources of knowledge. It is the Self that functions through them. Similarly, the objects of the world which are inert cannot become manifest by themselves. It is by the reflection of the Self's luminosity that they become manifest.

Nescience, *avidyā*, is not opposed to the Self, as was stated above; it is itself made manifest by the Self. But, the reflection of the Self which is consciousness in the internal organ is what removes nescience. A pot, for instance, is not known as long as a cognitive mode of the mind carrying the reflection of consciousness does not pervade it. As soon as the pervasion takes place, the ignorance veiling the pot is removed, and the pot is known. As regards internal modes of the mind such as desire or anger, there is no need for pervasion by another mental mode, because they are themselves modes of the mind carrying the reflection of consciousness, and are manifest as long as they last. Things like pot, cloth, etc., exist as superimposed on the Self; but they do not become manifest until a mental mode pervades them and reveals them. The mental mode flows out through the channel of the sense-organs such as the eyes, pervades the object occasioning a reflection of consciousness. This brings about the identity of the reflection of consciousness within, in the mind, and the reflection in the object. This is what makes the object manifest. Thus, there is no unintelligibility in our statement that the Self is not opposed to nescience. What is opposed to it is the cognitive mode of the mind.

There is a view which holds that the Self is inert and that by the knowledge which is located in it the objects like pot become manifest. This view is unintelligible because there cannot be any relation such as conjunction between the knowledge that resides in the Self, whether that knowledge be inert or self-luminous, and the objects like pot. If it be said that its very nature is the relation (*svarūpasaṁbandha*), then since the relation is always there, every object should be manifest always, which is not the case.

According to another view, the object becomes manifest of its own accord, since manifestation belongs to it. This view also is unacceptable. If manifestation belongs to the object, there can be no relation between the object and the Self. In the absence of this relation, the notion "I know" which implies the cognitive relation between the Self and the object would be unintelligible.

Thus, our view stands vindicated. It is by the relation of pot, etc., with the self-luminous witness-consciousness that they become manifest. The entire world shines as illuminated by the Self which is pure consciousness. Even the so-called luminaries like the sun and the stars shine only by borrowed light. The splendour of the world is a reflected glory. The ground of all manifestation is Self-awareness. It is this truth which Śrī Dakṣiṇāmūrti teaches.

5

देहं प्राणमपीन्द्रियाण्यपि चलां बुद्धिं च शून्यं विदुः
स्त्रीबालान्धजडोपमास्त्वहमिति भ्रान्ता भृशं वादिनः ।
मायाशक्तिविलासकल्पितमहाव्यामोहसंहारिणे
तस्मै श्रीगुरुमूर्तये नम इदं श्रीदक्षिणामूर्तये ॥

deham prāṇam apīndriyāṇyapi calāṁ buddhiṁ ca śūnyaṁ viduḥ
strībālāndhajaḍopamās tvaham iti bhrāntā bhṛśaṁ vādinaḥ|
māyā-śakti-vilāsa-kalpita mahāvyāmoha-saṁhāriṇe
tasmai śrī-gurumūrtaye nama idaṁ śrī-dakṣiṇāmūrtaye||

They who know the 'I' as body, breath, senses the changing intellect, or the void, are deluded like women and children, and the blind and the stupid and talk much. To Him who destroys the great delusion posited by the sport of *māyā's* power: to Him of the form of the Preceptor, the blessed Dakṣiṇāmūrti may this obeisance be !

Many are the philosophies of the Self. Although they agree that there is the Self, they differ widely over the question, what is the Self. The materialists identify the Self with the physical body. There are some who think that the senses constitute the Self. The vitalists contend that the vital breath is the Self. The subjective idealists resolve the Self into a flux of momentary ideas. The nihilists say that the Self is nothing.

The materialists say that the basis for all empirical usage is the physical body. It is the body that is the Self. All that has been stated in the previous verses is like doing a mural painting without the wall. Like the wall which is the basis for the painting, the body is the substrate of all our experiences. When I say, "I walk", "I stay", "I am stout", "I am lean", etc., what I refer to as "I" is the physical body. Therefore, it is the physical body that is the Self.

Another section of the materialists, who are more refined than the materialists in general, contend that it is not the physical body but the sense-organs that constitute the Self. The evidence that is cited in support of this view is such empirical usage as "I speak", "I see", "I hear", etc.

A still other section, whose intellects have gained a little more purity, hold that the vital principle (*prāṇa*) is the Self. Even after the loss of sense-organs, one is seen to be active. And so, it is the vital principle that is the self. There is also the evidence provided by such experience as "I am hungry", "I am thirsty", etc.; hunger, thirst, etc., are functions of the vital principle.

The mentalists believe that the mind (*manas*) is the Self. The vital air, like the air that is without, is also inert; and so it cannot be the Self; it cannot be that which enjoys or experiences. It is the mind that is the conscious enjoyer. And so, that alone is the Self.

The Yogācāra view is that the mind of the individual cannot be the Self, because one says "my mind", implying a distinction between "I" and mind, and that the Self is a series of momentary cognitions (*kṣaṇikavijñāna*), as one's experience is that the Self is of the nature of changing consciousness, a flux of cognitions.

What is ceaselessly changing and momentary like the lightning or the winking of the eyes, cannot be the Self. And so, the Śūnyavādin says that there is no Self at all. In deep sleep there is nothing, there is void—neither the subject of experience nor objects of experience. If one must use the expression 'Self', it can only refer to 'nothing'.

Every one of these views is born of misapprehension, because reflection will reveal that the physical body, etc., cannot be the Self. Whatever is inert, whatever is an object of knowledge, whatever contradicts itself, cannot be the Self which is of the nature of consciousness. Such views, therefore, are engendered by *avidyā* (nescience). Those who hold such views are compared to 'women', 'children', the 'blind', and the 'stupid'. Here the term 'women' stands for a type of character which is narrow and possessive—the character that is represented in the *Bṛhadāraṇyaka-upaniṣad* by Kātyāyanī and not by Maitreyī. It is obvious that such a type of character is to be found among the so-called men too. The word 'children' refers to immaturity. The expression 'blind' and 'stupid' are privative terms. The purpose of the comparison is to teach that the wrong views of the Self are due to delusion.

How is this delusion to be removed? By the grace of the Guru Dakṣiṇāmūrti. It is He that destroys *māyā*, the power of delusion, which puts up the show-world of plurality, with aspects of which the disputants identify the Self.

6

राहुग्रस्तदिवाकरेन्दुसदृशो मायासमाच्छादनात्
सन्मात्रः करणोपसंहरणतो योऽभूत्सुषुप्तः पुमान् ।
प्रागस्वाप्समिति प्रबोधसमये यः प्रत्यभिज्ञायते
तस्मै श्रीगुरुमूर्तये नम इदं श्रीदक्षिणामूर्तये ॥

rāhu-grasta-divākarendu-sadṛśo māyā-samācchādanāt
san-mātraḥ karaṇopasaṁharaṇato yobhūt-suṣuptaḥ pumān|
prāgasvāpsam iti prabodha-samaye yaḥ pratyabhijñāyate
tasmai śrī-gurumūrtaye nama idaṁ-śrī-dakṣiṇāmūrtaye||

To the Self, who in sleep becomes pure Existence, on the withdrawal of the veiling by *māyā*, like unto the sun or the moon, in eclipse, and on waking recognizes, 'I have slept till now' to Him, of the form of the Preceptor, the blessed Dakṣiṇāmūrti, may this obeisance be !

It is not true to say that in deep sleep there is nothing. In that state, the instruments of cognition do not function. Yet, the Self remains as pure existence-consciousness-bliss. It is not proper to build a philosophy, ignoring the evidence provided by deep sleep experience. The various systems seek to structure their philosophies on the foundations provided by only one aspect of experience, viz, waking. Advaita examines experience as a whole in its triple form — waking, dreaming, and sleep. The evidence of sleep is of special importance, because it reveals a truth which is otherwise unobtainable by us. Sleep is not a state of emptiness. While in waking and dreaming, consciousness is related to a world of objects and images, in sleep it shines as Existence unrelated to anything else. It is also evident that consciousness is not to be regarded as a characteristic of the mind, because in sleep there is no mind, and yet there is consciousness. That there is consciousness in sleep is clear because on waking up we say, 'I slept happily; I did not know anything.' Just as consciousness is required for knowing the presence of anything, even so it must be there for knowing the absence of all things. Sleep also shows that the Self which is pure consciousness is not realised as such because of the veil of *māyā.* This is compared to the solar or lunar eclipse. The comparison with the solar eclipse is particularly significant. Even during the eclipse the sun shines without any change. It is our vision of the sun that is obstructed by the interposition of the moon. So, the Self does not suffer, in truth, by *māyā*. It is our view that is mutilated and distorted. And it is this mutilated and distorted vision that is removed by the Preceptor Dakṣiṇāmūrti by His teaching.

7

बाल्यादिष्वपि जाग्रदादिषु तथा सर्वास्ववस्थास्वपि
व्यावृत्तास्वनुवर्तमानमहमित्यन्तः स्फुरन्तं सदा ।
स्वात्मानं प्रकटीकरोति भजतां यो मुद्रया भद्रया
तस्मै श्रीगुरुमूर्तये नम इदं श्रीदक्षिणामूर्तये ॥

bālyādiṣvapi jāgradādiṣu tathā sarvāsvavasthāsvapi
vyāvṛttāsvanuvartamānam-aham-ity-antaḥ sphurantaṁ sadā/
svātmānaṁ prakaṭīkaroti bhajatāṁ yo mudrayā bhadrayā
tasmai Śrī-gurumūrtaye nama idaṁ Śrī-dakṣiṇāmūrtaye//

To Him who, by means of the blessed hand-pose, manifests to His devotees His own Self that, for ever, shines within as 'I', constantly, in all the inconstant states such as infancy, etc., and waking, etc., to Him, of the form of the Preceptor, the blessed Dakṣiṇāmūrti, may this obeisance be !

Here is taught the method of enquiring into the nature of the Self. The method consists in recognising the Self that is constant and unvarying in the inconstant and varying states in which it is found. Recognition is a process whereby identity is discovered in spite of differences. The usual example given of recognition is 'This is that Devadatta'. I recognise here that the Devadatta whom I see now and in front of me is the same Devadatta whom I saw on a previous day elsewhere. Setting aside the differences of time and place, I recognise the identity of person. Similarly, the Self is to be realised as the same unchanging reality in the states that keep on changing. As examples of the changing states are given those that pertain to a life-span and those that occur every day. Infancy, adolescence, etc., waking, dream, etc., have their own peculiarities and respective time-periods. The body in each case changes; so do the mind and the world too. What is taken to be real in one condition is seen to be unreal in another. What dominates one state disappears in the others. But what persists in every state without itself changing is the Self. It neither rises nor sets. It is the eternal, immutable, pure consciousness.

This is the meaning: The states, which are illusory, inert, and of the nature of misery, change and pass away. But the Self persists in all of them as the constant imperishable witness. When, for instance, waking supervenes on dream, one recalls thus, "I who was dreaming am awake now." Similarly, when one grows out of childhood and becomes an adult, one does not lose sight of identity. One recalls: 'I who was a child am now a grown up man." And so it is with experiences like seeing and hearing: "It is the same 'I' that saw then that is now hearing." The states of experience change, but the "I" persists: the stages in one's life change, but the "I" persists. Likewise, the objects of pleasure and enjoyment change, but the "I" persists. The "I" is the witness of all experiences, their basic and unchanging reality. It is existence, consciousness, happiness. It is the inmost being, self luminous awareness, the seat and centre of supreme bliss. It shines always as the "I" within.

It is this truth which Śrī Dakṣiṇāmūrti teaches by means of the hand-pose known as the *cin-mudrā*, the symbol of pure consciousness. In this pose, the thumb and the index finger of the right hand are joined at their tips while the other three fingers stand apart. The significance of this pose is that there is identity in the midst of apparent diversity.

8

विश्वं पश्यति कार्यकारणतया स्वस्वामिसंबन्धतः
शिष्याचार्यतया तथैव पितृपुत्राद्यात्मना भेदतः ।

स्वप्ने जाग्रति वा य एष पुरुषो मायापरिभ्रामितः
तस्मै श्रीगुरुमूर्तये नम इदं श्रीदक्षिणामूर्तये ॥

viśvaṁ paśyati kārya-kāraṇatayā sva-svāmi-saṁbandhataḥ
śiṣyācāryatayā tathaiva pitṛ-putrādy-ātmanā bhedataḥ|
svapne jāgrati vā ya eṣa puruṣo māyā-paribhrāmitaḥ
tasmai śrī-gurumūrtaye nama idaṁ śrī-dakṣiṇātmūrtaye||

To the Self who, deluded by *māyā* sees, in dreaming and waking, the universe in its distinctions, such as cause and effect, property and proprietor, disciple and teacher, and father and son, likewise—to Him, of the form of the Preceptor, the blessed Dakṣiṇāmūrti may this obeisance be!

If there is no reality other than the Self, then how is instruction of the supreme truth possible? Also, how can there be anyone in bondage? Instruction in knowledge for the sake of removing bondage would be intelligible only if there are bound souls! Nor is it possible that there are released souls endowed with knowledge; for, there are no *guru*, scripture, etc., as the sources of knowledge effecting release?

To such questions, the present verse gives the answer.

All empirical usage is grounded in *māyā* which is beginningless, indeterminable, and is superimposed on the supreme Self. *Māyā* is there till the onset of Self-knowledge. Although, in truth, there is no plurality, the *jīva* perceives plurality on account of *māyā*.

The universe involving distinctions is a manifestation of *māyā*. What exists and what is real is the one and the only Self. But on account of *māyā* there is the appearance of plurality. All relations fall within *māyā*. All empirical usage is founded on *māyā*. For instance, the causal relation serves practical purposes. Without it the phenomenal world would be unintelligible. But if we inquire into the nature of the causal relation itself, we shall discover that that relation, as all relations, is unintelligible. Is the effect different from its cause, or is it identical therewith? Either way, there is difficulty. Is there a first cause, and is there an ultimate effect ? Both the positions involve self-contradiction. Thus, no relation is intelligible. Relations such as those between master and servant, father and son, teacher and disciple, obtain only in *māyā*. In the states of waking and dreaming, one experiences these relations. These relations are not constant, nor are they concordant as between the two states. Just as the dream relations are illusory, the waking relations are also so. There is no world *of* the Self: for there is no world apart from the Self. One speaks of the head *of* Rāhu, the emptiness of ether, *my* self, the body *of* an idol, etc. In each of these cases, there is no real possessive relation corresponding to the expression: for Rāhu is the head, ether is emptiness, I am the Self, and the idol is the body. Similarly, the relations that are predicated of the Self have no reality, for the Self alone is real.

How the illusory preceptor, scripture, etc., destroy the illusory world of plurality and lead the soul to release may thus be illustrated. A man is having a pleasant dream. He sees beautiful sights, meets intimate friends, comes by fascinating things. All of a sudden a ferocious tiger runs towards him, threatening to eat him up. This wakes him up from his dream. The dream-tiger is no less illusory than the other dream-contents. But it serves as the sublator of the entire dream, including itself. Similarly, the preceptor, scripture, etc., although projections of *māyā*, serve to remove *māyā*, by bestowing knowledge. He who has gained knowledge in this way, is deluded no longer. He remains eternally as the non-dual Self.

In his *Saṁkṣepa-śārīraka*, Sarvajñātma-muni says:

"Know, therefore, that *Brahman* attains, through nescience, the status of the *jīva* and remains as of your nature, and that you see the entire universe from ether to earth, projected by your mind."

"Preceptor, *Veda*, *Brahma-sūtra*, etc., are posited by nescience. From them arises knowledge for the *jīva*. When, by that knowledge, delusion has been destroyed, it stays in its own true nature as the self-luminous Self." (ii, 162-163)

9

भूरम्भांस्यनलोनिलोम्बरमहर्नाथो हिमांशुः पुमा-
नित्याभाति चराचरात्मकमिदं यस्यैव मूर्त्यष्टकम् ।

नान्यत्किञ्चन विद्यते विमृशतां यस्मात्परस्माद्विभो-
स्तस्मै श्रीगुरुमूर्तये नम इदं श्रीदक्षिणामूर्तये ॥

bhūr ambhāṁsyanalo'nilo'mbaram aharnātho himāṁśuḥ pumān
ityābhāti carācarātmakam idaṁ yasyaiva mūrty-aṣṭakam/
nānyat kiñcana vidyate vimṛśatāṁ yasmāt parasmād vibhoḥ
tasmai śrī-gurumūrtaye nama idaṁ śrī-dakśiṇāmūrtaye//

To Him whose eightfold form is all this moving and unmoving universe, appearing as earth, water fire, air, ether, the sun, the moon and soul: beyond whom, supreme and all-pervading, there exists nought else for those who enquire—to Him, of the form of the Preceptor, the blessed Dakṣiṇāmūrti may this obeisance be !

For realising *Brahman*, the means prescribed for the lower grades of aspirants is the meditation on God in His eightfold form (*aṣṭamūrta*). The means for those who are of the top-grade is inquiry into the purport of Vedānta through hearing, reflection, and contemplation. This is taught in the present verse.

Brahman as endowed with attributes is *Īśvara* (God). *Īśvara* is the whole and sole cause of the world. He becomes the cause of the world through his power called *māyā*. The world of the living and the non-living, the sentient and the insentient, is an illusory manifestation of *māyā*. The macrocosm and the microcosm are made of the same stuff. What is without is within as well. The number of principles (*tattvas*) constituting the world-process is different according to different systems of thought. Śaivism enumerates thirty-six principles. Of these, eight are the easily recognisable ones. The five elements, the sun and the moon and soul form the body of God, as it were. Śiva is *aṣṭa-mūrta* (of eight-fold form). It is thus that he is immanent in the universe. He is *viśva-māyā* (of the form of the universe). He is to be worshipped thus.

The worshipper should meditate on the oneness of the individual being and the cosmic form. The individual body is made of the five elements. So is the cosmos. It should be realised that all are one—the five elements, the vital airs, the sun, the moon, etc. Identifying the individual soul endowed with the body made of five elements with the supreme Lord who is of eightfold form, the worshipper should contemplate the supreme Identity of the form "I am Sadāśiva".

By the strength of the Identity-contemplation, the aspirant gains oneness with the Lord, becomes endowed with lordly splendour, and finally is released through the knowledge bestowed by divine grace.

The teaching about the *saguṇa-Brahman* or *Īśvara* and world-process has for its purport the transcendence of duality. The Real in itself, the pure Absolute, is the non-dual Self. There are no distinctions in and for it. There is nothing apart from it. Those who enquire will realise that *Brahman* alone is real. The Self is not exhausted by the world; it is *viśvādhika* (more than the world). It is *niṣprapañca* (void of the universe). Since the world is an appearance, it has no reality other than that of *Brahman.* While the ignorant believe that that world is real, the wise know that there is nothing other than *Brahman.*

In the *Śivamahimna-stava* it is said:

"Thou art the Sun, Thou the Moon; Thou art Air; Thou art Fire; Thou art Water, Ether, Earth; and Thou art the Self. Thus they declare, restricting Thy nature. But, we do not know here of any principle that Thou dost not become". (26)

The aspirants of the top grade realise the non-duality of *Brahman*, and gain release here itself, which consists in remaining as the supreme Śiva, of the nature of existence-consciousness-bliss.

It is this plenary truth that is taught by Śrī Dakṣiṇāmūrti who is the preceptor-form of the absolute Self.

10

सर्वात्मत्वमितिस्फुटीकृतमिदं यस्मादमुष्मिस्तवे
तेनास्य श्रवणात्तदर्थमननाद्ध्यानाच्च सङ्कीर्तनात् ।
सर्वात्मत्वमहाविभूतिसहितं स्यादीश्वरत्वं स्वतः
सिद्ध्येत्तत्पुनरष्टधा परिणतं चैश्वर्यमव्याहतम् ॥

sarvātmatvam iti sphuṭīkṛtam idaṁ yasmād amuṣmiṁ stave
tenāsya śravaṇāt tadartha-mananād dhyānācca saṅkīrtanāt|
sarvātmatva-mahāvibhūtisahitaṁ syād īśvaratvaṁ svataḥ
siddhyet tat punar aṣṭadhā pariṇataṁ caiśvaryam avyāhatam||

Since, in this hymn, the All-Self-hood has thus been explained, by hearing this, by reflecting on its meaning, by meditating on it, and by reciting, there will naturally come about lordship (*Īśvaratva*) together with the supreme splendour consisting in All-Self-hood; and will be achieved, again, the unimpeded supernormal power presenting itself in eight forms.

The fruit of Vedānta is All-Self-hood (*sarvātmatva*). The meaning of this expression is not that there is an "All" which is pervaded by the Self, but that the Self is All. It is this truth that is taught in the Hymn to Dakṣiṇāmūrti.

The way to understand it consists of *śravaṇa*, *manana*, and *nididhyāsana*. One has to study the text, reflect on its meaning, and contemplate the truth taught therein. At the end of this process one realises the Self. There is no goal which is higher than this. All other ends, including the acquisition of the supernormal powers, are included in it. It is only till the Self is realised that the other objectives seem important and worthwhile. It is only a figure of speech to say, 'Seek ye the Self, and all other things will be added unto you'. For, if the Self is sought and gained, there will be nothing else to be added.

चित्रं वटतरोर्मूले वृद्धाः शिष्या: गुरुर्युवा ।
गुरोस्तु मौनं व्याख्यानं शिष्यास्तु छिन्नसंशया: ।।

citraṁ vaṭataror-mūle vṛddhāḥ śiṣyāḥ gurur-yuvā|
guros-tu maunaṁ vyākhyānaṁ śiṣyās-tu chinna-saṁśayāḥ||

A wonderful picture! Beneath the banyan tree, the disciples are old, and the preceptor is young. The instruction given by the preceptor is in silence; and the doubts of the disciples are dispelled.

ब्रह्मादिदेववन्द्याय सर्वलोकाश्रयाय ते ।
दक्षिणामूर्तिरूपाय शङ्कराय नमो नमः ॥

brahmādi-deva-vandyāya sarva-lokāśrayāya te/
dakṣiṇāmūrti-rūpāya śaṅkarāya namo namaḥ//

To You who are adored by the gods, Brahmā and others, and who are the support of all the worlds, to You who bear the form of Dakṣiṇāmūrti, the bestower of blessedness — obeisance, obeisance!

II

HYMN TO GURU

॥ श्रीः ॥

जन्मानेकशतैः सदादरयुजा भक्त्या समाराधितो
भक्तैर्वैदिकलक्षणेन विधिना सन्तुष्ट ईशः स्वयम् ।
साक्षाच्छ्रीगुरुरूपमेत्य कृपया दृग्गोचरः सन् प्रभुः
तत्त्वं साधु विबोध्य तारयति तान् संसारदुःखार्णवात् ॥

janmānekaśataiḥ sadādarayujā bhaktyā samārādhito
bhaktairvaidikalakṣaṇena vidhinā santuṣṭa īśaḥ svayam|
sākṣācchrīgururūpametya kṛpayā dṛggocaraḥ san prabhuḥ
tattvaṁ sādhu vibodhya tārayati tān saṁsāraduhkhārṇavāt||

The Supreme Lord, being pleased by the reverent and devout worship of his devotees according to the scriptural injunctions in their innumerable previous births, incarnates Himself, out of compassion, in the form of a Preceptor, thereby comes within the range of perception, well imparts to them the knowledge of the Ultimate Reality and makes them transcend the Ocean of misery consisting of the phenomenal existence.

॥ गर्वष्टकम् ॥

GURVAṢṬAKAM

A Hymn of Eight Verses in Praise of the Guru

The theme of this poem, which is sweet both in sound and sense, is the need for devotion to the *Guru*. Even the choicest blessings of the world are as nothing before the grace of the *Guru*. One may have all the excellences of body, mind, and spirit : but if one has not earned the *Guru's* grace, nothing will avail one. The means to receive the blessings of the *Guru* is unwavering devotion to Him. Hence Ācārya Śaṅkara makes this the burden of his poem: nothing will accrue from anything, however great or noble it may be, if the mind is not engaged in devotion to the *Guru*.

The ninth verse is in praise of the octad (*phala-śruti*).

1

शरीरं सुरूपं तथा वा कलत्रं
यशश्चारु चित्रं धनं मेरुतुल्यम् ।
मनश्चेन्न लग्नं गुरोरङ्घ्रिपद्मे
ततः किं ततः किं ततः किं ततः किम् ॥

śarīraṁ surūpaṁ tathā vā kalatraṁ
yaśaścāru citraṁ dhanaṁ merutulyam/
manaścenna lagnaṁ guroraṅghripadme
tataḥ kiṁ tataḥ kiṁ tataḥ kiṁ tataḥ kim//

One's body may be handsome, wife beautiful, fame excellent and varied, and wealth like unto Mount Meru; but if one's mind be not attached to the lotus feet of the *Guru*, what thence, what thence, what thence, what thence?

2

कलत्रं धनं पुत्रपौत्रादि सर्वं
गृहं बान्धवाः सर्वमेतद्धि जातम् ।

मनश्चेन्न लग्नं गुरोरङ्घ्रिपद्मे
ततः किं ततः किं ततः किं ततः किम् ॥

kalatraṁ dhanaṁ putrapautrādi sarvaṁ
gṛhaṁ bāndhavāḥ sarvametaddhi jātam/
manaścenna lagnaṁ guroraṅghripadme
tataḥ kiṁ tataḥ kiṁ tataḥ kiṁ tataḥ kim//

Wife, wealth, sons, grandsons, etc., all these; home, relations—the host of all these there may be; but if one's mind be not attached to the lotus feet of the *Guru*, what thence, what thence, what thence, what thence?

3

षडङ्गादिवेदो मुखे शास्त्रविद्या
कवित्वादि गद्यं सुपद्यं करोति ।
मनश्चेन्न लग्नं गुरोरङ्घ्रिपद्मे
ततः किं ततः किं ततः किं ततः किम् ॥

ṣaḍaṅgādivedo mukhe śāstravidyā
kavitvādi gadyaṁ supadyaṁ karoti/
manaścenna lagnaṁ guroraṅghripadme
tataḥ kiṁ tataḥ kiṁ tataḥ kiṁ tataḥ kim//

The Vedas with their six auxiliaries and knowledge of sciences may be on one's lips; one may have the gift of poesy; and may compose good prose and poetry; but if one's mind be not attached to the lotus feet of the *Guru*, what thence, what thence, what thence, what thence?

4

विदेशेषु मान्यः स्वदेशेषु धन्यः
सदाचारवृत्तेषु मत्तो न चान्यः ।
मनश्चेन्न लग्नं गुरोरङ्घ्रिपद्मे
ततः किं ततः किं ततः किं ततः किम् ॥

videśeṣu mānyaḥ svadeśeṣu dhanyaḥ
sadācāravṛtteṣu matto na cānyaḥ|
manaścenna lagnaṁ gurоraṅghripadme
tataḥ kiṁ tataḥ kiṁ tataḥ kiṁ tataḥ kim||

'In other lands I am honoured; in my country I am fortunate; in the ways of good conduct there is none that excels me'—thus one may think; but if one's mind be not attached to the lotus feet of the *Guru*, what thence, what thence, what thence, what thence?

5

क्षमामण्डले भूपभूपालवृन्दैः
सदा सेवितं यस्य पादारविन्दम् ।
मनश्चेन्न लग्नं गुरोरङ्घ्रिपद्मे
ततः किं ततः किं ततः किं ततः किम् ॥

kṣamāmaṇḍale bhūpabhūpālavṛndaiḥ
sadā sevitaṁ yasya pādāravindam|
manaścenna lagnaṁ gurоraṅghripadme
tataḥ kiṁ tataḥ kiṁ tataḥ kiṁ tataḥ kim||

One's feet may be adored constantly by hosts of emperors and kings of the world; but if one's mind be not attached to the lotus feet of the *Guru*, what thence, what thence, what thence, what thence?

6

यशो मे गतं दिक्षु दानप्रतापा-
ज्जगद्वस्तु सर्वं करे यत्प्रसादात् ।
मनश्चेन्न लग्नं गुरोरङ्घ्रिपद्मे
ततः किं ततः किं ततः किं ततः किम् ॥

yaśo me gataṁ dikṣu dānapratāpāj-
jagadvastu sarvaṁ kare yatprasādāt/
manaścenna lagnaṃ guroraṅghripadme
tataḥ kiṁ tataḥ kiṁ tataḥ kiṁ tataḥ kim//

My fame has spread in all quarters by virtue of generosity and prowess; all the things of the world are in my hands as a reward of these virtues; but if one's mind be not attached to the lotus feet of the *Guru*, what thence, what thence, what thence, what thence?

7

न भोगे न योगे न वा वाजिराजौ
न कान्तामुखे नैव वित्तेषु चित्तम् ।
मनश्चेन्न लग्नं गुरोरङ्घ्रिपद्मे
ततः किं ततः किं ततः किं ततः किम् ॥

na bhoge na yoge na vā vājirājau
na kāntāmukhe naiva vitteṣu cittam/
manaścenna lagnaṁ guroraṅghripadme
tataḥ kiṁ tataḥ kiṁ tataḥ kiṁ tataḥ kim//

Not in enjoyment, not in concentration, not in the multitudes of horses; nor in the face of the beloved, nor in wealth does the mind dwell; but if that mind be not attached to the lotus feet of the *Guru,* what thence, what thence, what thence, what thence ?

8

अरण्ये न वा स्वस्य गेहे न कार्ये
न देहे मनो वर्तते मे त्वनर्घ्ये ।
मनश्चेन्न लग्नं गुरोरङ्घ्रिपद्मे
ततः किं ततः किं ततः किं ततः किम् ॥

araṇye na vā svasya gehe na kārye
na dehe mano vartate me tvanarghye|
manaścenna lagnaṁ guroraṅghripadme
tataḥ kiṁ tataḥ kiṁ tataḥ kiṁ tataḥ kim||

Not in the forest, nor even in one's own house, nor in what-is-to-be-accomplished, nor in the body, nor in what is invaluable does my mind dwell; but if my mind be not attached to the lotus feet of the *Guru*, what thence, what thence, what thence, what thence ?

9

गुरोरष्टकं यः पठेत्पुण्यदेही
यतिर्भूपतिर्ब्रह्मचारी च गेही ।
लभेद्वाञ्छितार्थं पदं ब्रह्मसंज्ञं
गुरोरुक्तवाक्ये मनो यस्य लग्नम् ॥

gurorаṣṭakaṁ yaḥ paṭhet-puṇyadehī
yatir-bhūpatir-brahmacārī ca gehī|
labhedvāñchitārthaṁ padaṁ brahmasaṁjñaṁ
guroruktavākye mano yasya lagnam||

That virtuous person who reads this octad on the *Guru*, and whose mind is fixed on the sayings of the *Guru*—whether he be an ascetic, king, student, or householder, attains the desired goal, the state which is called *Brahman*.

PLATE 3

Śrī Govinda

(Facing p. 33)

III

BHAJA GOVINDAM

INTRODUCTION

There is a story attached to the composition of the present Hymn. Ācārya Śaṅkara, it is said, was walking along a street in Vārāṇasī, one day, accompanied by his disciples. He heard the sound of grammatical rules being recited by an old scholar. Taking pity on the scholar, he went up to him and advised him not to waste his time on grammar but to turn his mind to God in worship and adoration. The *Hymn to Govinda* was composed on this occasion. Besides the refrain of the song beginning with the words *bhaja govindam*, Śaṅkara is stated to have sung twelve verses; hence the hymn bears the title *Dvādaśamañjarikā-stotra* (A hymn which is a bunch of twelve verse-blossoms). The fourteen disciples who were with the Master, then, are believed to have added one verse each: these fourteen verses are together called *Caturdaśa-mañjarikā-stotra* (A hymn which is a bunch of fourteen verse-blossoms). In some editions the two sets are given separately, with a verse added at the end of each wherein the authorship and the occasion are mentioned. Apart from minor variant readings, there are quite a few variations among the editions. One half of a verse, in some cases, is combined with a half of another verse. The order in which the verses appear is not quite the same in all the editions. Certain additional verses also occur in the generally accepted form of the hymn. These additions are sometimes referred to as the 'surplus' (*śeṣa*).

The text that is presented here follows the one printed in volume 18 (pages 62-69) of the Memorial Edition of *The Works of Śrī Śaṅkarācārya*, published by Sri Vani Vilas Press, Srirangam, with a few minor variant readings adopted from other printed editions. The text consists of thirty-one verses including the refrain beginning with the words *bhaja govindam*, and bears the title *Mohamudgara*, which means 'the hammer that strikes at delusion'. Popularly the hymn is referred to as *Bhaja Govindam.*

There is a manuscript commentary, *Dvādaśamañjarikā-vivaraṇa*, by one Svayaṁprakāśa Svāmin (Government Oriental Manuscripts Library, Madras; No. D.10067). In the invocatory verses, the commentator Svayaṁprakāśa offers obeisance to Śrī Svaprakāśa, the lord of the world (*viśveśa*), to Śrī Rāma, his chosen deity (*iṣṭa*) and to Śrī Gopāla-Yogīndra, his preceptor. The first three invocatory verses read as follows:

(1) *yatpāda-smaraṇaṁ samasta-jagatāṁ sarvārthasiddhi-pradaṁ*
yannāma-śravaṇaṁ viśuddha-manasāṁ jñāna-pradaṁ yogināṁ/
yatkāruṇya-kaṭākṣa-vīkṣaṇam aho saṁsārasaṁtāraṇaṁ
taṁ viśveśam anantam ādyam amalaṁ śrī-svaprakāśaṁ bhaje//

(2) *sarvādhāram anādhāraṁ sargasthityanta-kāriṇam/*
sarvajñaṁ karuṇāmūrtiṁ śrī rāmaṁ śaraṇaṁ bhaje//

(3) *yatprasādād-ahaṁ sākṣād-īśvarāṇām apīśvaraḥ/*
śrīmad-gopālayogīndrāṁś tān vande karuṇānidhīn//

The next verse is in praise of Śrī Śaṅkara. Svayaṁprakāśa says here that his own words (in the form of the commentary) have become valuable because of their connection with the Ācārya's work, the *Dvādaśa-mañjarikā*, even as the drain-water becomes sacred when it joins the Gaṅgā:

ācāryakṛti-saṁbandhān-madvākyaṁ
ślāghyam eva hi/
rathyodakaṁ yathā gaṅgāpravāha-
patanāc-chubham//

According to Svayaṁprakāśa, the *Dvādaśamañjarikā* is a *prakaraṇa* work, a manual of *Advaita-Vedānta.* He does not call it a *stotra* (hymn). It is significant that the refrain beginning with the words *bhaja govindam* is not found in the manuscript commentary. Nor is there any reference to the grammarian and his recitation. In some printed editions, as already stated, there is a verse added at the end of the twelve verses attributed to Śaṅkara (thirteen including the refrain), wherein are mentioned the authorship and the occasion of the composition. The verse reads thus:

dvādaśamañjarikābhir-aśeṣaḥ
kathito vaiyākaraṇasyaiṣaḥ/
upadeśo' bhūd-vidyānipuṇaiḥ
śrīmacchaṅkarabhagavaccaraṇaiḥ//

[Through the twelve verse-blossoms, all this entire teaching was imparted to the grammarian by the most wise Śrī Śaṅkara-bhagavat-pāda.]

Instead of the above verse, Svayaṁprakāśa has the following:

dvādaśamañjarikābhir-aśeṣaḥ
śiṣyāṇāṁ kathito hyupadeśaḥ/
yeṣān-naiva karoti vivekaṁ
te pacyante narakam anekam//

[Through the twelve verse-blossoms, the entire teaching was imparted to the disciples. Those for whom this teaching does not bring discriminative wisdom will suffer in many a hell.]

Svayaṁprakāśa's commentary is on exactly twelve verses. The verses occur in the following order: 2, 29, 8, 4, 11, 3, 18, 26, 12, 13, 24, ab+25 cd, and 17. (These numbers refer to the places of the verses in the present edition). Hence the title *Dvādaśamañjarikā* does strictly apply to this collection. Explaining the meaning of the title, Svayaṁprakāśa says: Just as a cluster of blossoms pleases the mind by a mere look, so also this manual purifies the mind by mere study through generating detachment and knowledge. Or, just as a cluster of blossoms pleases the bees through honey, even so this manual brings satisfaction to the disciples. Hence the comparison of the manual to a cluster of blossoms is quite apt. (*yathā mañjarikā avalokanamātreṇa cittaṁ prasādayati, evaṁ prakaraṇam api śravaṇamātrād eva vairāgya-jñānadvārā cittaṁ prasādayati. athavā mañjarī makarandadvārā yathā bhramarān prīṇayati, tathā śiṣyān prīṇayati. tasmān mañjarīsāmyaṁ prakaraṇasyopapannam eva*).

The method of exposition that a teacher adopts when he has to instruct his pupils is quite different from the one which he employs in order to convince or silence his opponents. Instruction (*upadeśa*) is different from disputation (*vāda*). The present manual is of the nature of instruction designed for the disciple. The word *śiṣya* (disciple, pupil) means: he who is *taught* by the teacher; he who becomes *distinguished* through knowledge of the texts, from the outward-turned individual that he was earlier; he who *restrains* the activity of the sense organs, etc. (Svayaṁprakāśa: *śikṣyata iti śiṣyaḥ, athavā śiṣyate viśiṣyate śāstrādi-parijñānena bahirmukhāpekṣayā iti śiṣyaḥ, athavā indriyādi-pravṛttiṁ śikṣayatīti śiṣyaḥ*).

The disciples are of two grades: those with impure mind (*vyākula-citta*), and those with pure mind (*avyākula-citta*). A disciple of the first category has a mind which is endowed with bad tendencies, passions, attachments etc., and is full of wild and vain imaginings. A disciple of the other category has no conceits—even those born of learning and good conduct—and no vanities, and is free from the habit of building castles in the air. Such a one gains release even by a single listening to the Vedāntic texts. But the other one has to first cleanse his mind and make it one pointed through the practice of *yoga*; and only thereafter will he get enlightened through Vedānta. The practicant of *yoga* may acquire super-normal powers. But these have nothing to do with realization. It cannot be said that it is only he that has these powers and can curse or bless people, is capable of realizing the Self. These extra-normal abilities are the fruits of *yoga*. They have no connection with *jñāna* (wisdom). The *jñānī* may also be a *yogī*. That, however, is a different matter. Thus, says Svayaṁprakāśa, realization is only through the study, etc., of Vedānta; the purification of the mind and meditation are but auxiliaries.

The present work is not meant for the disputants because it does not contain any dialectic. The Materialists (Cārvākas), and others do not accept the authority of Scripture. With reference to them, Svayaṁprakāśa relates the story of the man who, deprived of his nose, set about preaching: 'Lo, you may behold the heavenly worlds if you cut off your nose! Come, follow me and enjoy looking at these worlds!' Some did follow him only to get disappointed. The disputes among the followers of the different schools, the commentator compares to the barkings of a dog at its own reflections in a hall of mirrors. So, the disciple is taught, there is no use in disputation: *Advaita* means *non-quarrel.* Let one first acquire faith in the teacher and the teaching. It is this which will lead one to perfection. The present work is admirably suited to instruct the disciples in the fundamentals of Vedānta. The omniscient Lord incarnated himself in the form of Śaṅkarācārya, observes Svayaṁprakāśa, and first and foremost taught dispassion which is the means to knowledge; and in this composition, he addresses the disciple who is his own external life and mind as it were, as 'O fool!', even as a father would his son, out of great compassion. (*bhagavān sarvajñaḥ śaṅkarācāryarūpeṇa avatīrya prathamaṁ jñānasādhanavairāgyam upadiśan paramakāruṇikatvena piteva svatanayaṁ bahiḥprāṇacittaṁ śiṣyaṁ saṁbodhayati—mūḍha...iti*).

BHAJA GOVINDAM

[*Moha-mudgara*]

1

भज गोविन्दं भज गोविन्दं
भज गोविन्दं मूढमते ।
संप्राप्ते सन्निहिते काले
न हि न हि रक्षति डुकृञ्करणे ॥

bhaja govindaṁ bhaja govindaṁ
bhaja govindaṁ mūḍhamate|
saṁprāpte sannihite kāle
na hi na hi rakṣati ḍukṛñkaraṇe||

Adore the Lord, adore the Lord, adore the Lord, O fool ! When the appointed time (for departure) comes, the repetition of grammatical rules will not, indeed, save you.

This is the refrain of the hymn, and is sung at the end of every one of the other verses, as at the commencement of the hymn. As we have already noted in the Introduction, this does not occur in Svayaṁprakāśa's commentary.

Here the disciple is asked to occupy his mind with God rather than with such secular pursuits as the learning of grammatical rules. The grammatical formula mentioned here, *ḍukṛñkaraṇe*, is from the *Dhātupāṭha* in Pāṇini's work on grammar. It stands for all grammatical formulas, and, in fact, for all secular pursuits that do not involve any occupation with God. In the *Chāndogya Upaniṣad*, the story is told of Nārada seeking instruction from Sanatkumāra. Sanatkumāra asks Nārada to tell him first what he knows already. Nārada gives a long list of the sciences and arts beginning with the four Vedas and going down to snake-charming and the fine arts. In this list a high place is given to grammar which is described as the Veda of the Vedas. It is so called because it is through grammar that one understands the Vedas by analysing the words, etc. (Śaṅkara: *vyākaraṇena hi padādi-vibhāgaśaḥ ṛgvedādayo jñāyante*). But all the disciplines, of which Nārada is a master, are characterized by Sanatkumāra as being but names. The Infinite, *bhūman*, exceeds these; it is in the Infinite that true happiness lies, not in the finite. Thus, grammar may be useful as a means for understanding the truth. But it ought not to be made an end in itself.

What would grammatical knowledge do when death comes? If even expertise in grammar or linguistic analysis will not give solace to one at the time of death, what will other disciplines do? What, then, should one do? Śaṅkara's answer, as is the answer of every sage-teacher, is: Adore the Lord! Bhagavān Ramaṇa says in the *Uḷḷadu Nāṛpadu* (Forty Verses on Existence): those people who have intense fear of death seek as their refuge only in the feet of the great Lord, who is without death and birth.* Attachment to what perishes is not the way to release; devotion to the Imperishable can be the only means. To imagine that the finite goods will save one is a delusion. Such a one's mind is deluded; he is a fool (*mūḍhamati*).

It is also a delusion to postpone thinking of God to the time of death. The thoughts that are dominant in one's life – it is these that will recur at the end. It is not possible to turn one's mind to God when death approaches, if one has not prepared oneself for it through repeated worship and devotion. Śrī Kṛṣṇa declares in the *Bhagavadgītā* (vii.5) '*And, at the time of death*, he who remembers Me alone and departs, leaving the body, attains My being: here there is no doubt.' The force of the word *And* (*ca*) is that unless one has been remembering God earlier, one cannot remember Him at the time of death. As Śaṅkarānanda explains, 'even earlier, and at the time of death' (*pūrvam apy antakāle ca*).

The name of God chosen for adoration in the present hymn is Govinda. Any other name of God will suit as well. A seer of the *Ṛgveda* proclaims: 'The truth is one, and the sages call it by various names; they call it Indra, Yama, or Mātariśvan' (I, clxiv, 46). Śrī Kṛṣṇa says in the *Bhagavadgītā* (vii, 21): 'Whichever devotee desires to worship whichever form of the deity with faith,—the particular mode of faith of that particular devotee, I strengthen'. Śaṅkarānanda, commenting on this verse, observes: any form of the deity may be worshipped; it may be Śiva, Viṣṇu, Indra, or any other (*śivaṁ vā viṣṇuṁ vāpīndram anyaṁ vā*).

Govinda is one of the names by which Śrī Kṛṣṇa is known. The name occurs twice in the *Viṣṇusahasranāma* (verses 33 and 71). In his commentary on this work, Śaṅkara gives the following meanings to the word *Govinda*: (1) He who finds or knows the earth, (2) He who is the lord of cattle, (3) He who confers speech, and (4) He who is known through the Vedānta texts. Explaining the meaning of the term *Govinda* occurring in the *Bhagavadgītā*, ii, 9, Śaṅkarānanda says, 'Govinda is so called because He is obtainable through the Vedānta texts alone'

*See the present writer's *Ramaṇa Maharshi and His Philosophy of Existence*—Sri Ramaṇasramam, Tiruvannamalai, 1949), pp. 28 ff.

(*gobhir-vedānta-vākyair eva vindyate labhyata iti govindaḥ*). In the light of these explanations, it is clear, *Govinda* stands for the highest reality, the ground of existence, the goal of life; in a word, *God.*

The word *bhaja* means 'adoration, service, worship' (*bhaja-sevāyām*). It indicates all the nine grades of devotion (1) listening to the glory of God (*śravaṇa*), (2) singing the praise of God (*kīrtana*), (3) thinking of God (*smaraṇa*), (4) adoring the feet of God (*pādasevana*), (5) offering worship to God (*arcana*), (6) making obeisance to God (*vandana*), (7) servitude to God (*dāsya*), (8) friendship with God (*sakhya*), and (9) self-gift to God (*ātmanivedana*).

The repetition of the phrase *bhaja govindam* thrice is for the sake of emphasis.

2

मूढ जहीहि धनागमतृष्णां
कुरु सद्बुद्धिं मनसि वितृष्णाम् ।
यल्लभसे निजकर्मोपात्तं
वित्तं तेन विनोदय चित्तम् ॥

mūḍha jahīhi dhanāgamatṛṣṇāṁ
kuru sadbuddhiṁ manasi vitṛṣṇām|
yal-labhase nijakarmopāttaṁ
vittaṁ tena vinodaya cittam||

O fool! leave off the desire for accumulation of wealth; create in the mind thoughts about Reality, devoid of passion. What you get—i.e. what you have achieved through your past deeds—with that, satisfy your mind.

One of the desires that depresses man and degrades him is the desire for wealth. Attachment to property is the source of endless worry. There is travail in acquiring property; there is strain in preserving it; and there is pain when it is lost. It is foolish to imagine that wealth will bring in happiness. Man is not satisfied with any amount of wealth (*Kaṭha Upaniṣad*, i, 27;

na vittena tarpaṇīyo manuṣyaḥ). In the world, it is not observed that the gain of wealth affords contentment to any (Śaṅkara: *na hi loke vittalābhaḥ kasyacit tṛptikaro dṛṣṭaḥ*). In the *Bṛhadāraṇyaka Upaniṣad*, Maitreyī puts this question to her husband Yājñavalkya: "Sir, if this entire earth filled with wealth were mine, would I be immortal through that?" Yājñavalkya replies "No", and adds: "Your life will be just like that of people of means; but there is no hope of immortality through wealth" (*amṛtatvasya tu nāśāsti vittena.* II, iv, 2). Even conceptually (*manasāpi*), says Śaṅkara, there is no hope of immortality through wealth-produced work. In his *Vārttika* on the present text, Sureśvara makes Maitreyī ask Yājñavalkya: "If wealth makes for immortality, why do you want to give it away?" Work, dependent on wealth, cannot be the means to release, even as fire is not the remedy for burning (*na karma kāraṇaṁ mukter nāgnis tāpasya bheṣajam*). And so, Maitreyī's request to her husband is: Please do not give me the material wealth that perishes. That Wealth which has no beginning, middle, nor end, that Wealth which does not get depleted through enjoyment—let that Wealth alone be given."

nādir nānto na madhyaṁ vā yasya vittasya vidyate|
bhoge na ca kṣayaṁ yāti tadeva vasu dīyatām||

In the present verse of the *Bhaja Govindam*, Śaṅkara reminds us of the futility of accumulation of material wealth. Passionate attachments vitiate the mind and render it unfit to receive the light of truth. Hence, the passions should be removed from the mind. One should cultivate dispassion and detachment. Non-thirst (*vitṛṣṇā*) should take the place of thirst (*tṛṣṇā*). When the mind has been emptied of all its passions and attachments, with what should it be filled? The answer is: with meditations on Reality; with thoughts about the Real (*sat*). The Real is that which is not altered by time; it is the eternal Self, the supreme God, *Brahman*. *Brahman* is eternal, pure, of the nature of consciousness, ever free; it is the truth, subtle, pure existence, all-pervading, non-dual, and the ocean of bliss. These ten expressions are used (in the *Saṁkṣepaśārīraka*) to indicate the nature of Reality.

The meaning of the present verse, so far, is: Leaving off the three desires (for son, wealth, and the world), be engaged diligently in listening to the Vedānta texts, reflecting on their meaning, and meditating on their truth (Svayaṁprakāśa: *eṣaṇātrayaṁ parityajya śravaṇa-mananānididhyāsanādiśīlo bhava ity-arthaḥ*).

If one has to give up acquiring wealth, how is one to live, it may be asked. The reply is: let him live with whatever comes to him as a result of his past *karma*. Let him offer the fruits of his present deeds to God, so that his mind may become pure. Let him subsist on whatever comes his way, without coveting.

The present verse, as we have seen, is the first in the text given in Svayaṁprakāśa's commentary. Usually at the commencement of a work, the author offers obeisance to the chosen deity or preceptor, and indicates the subject-matter, aim etc., of the work. According to Svayaṁprakāśa, Śaṅkara the author of this work does this by using the word *sat* (in *kuru sad-buddhim*). By this word, observes the commentator, Śaṅkara performs the *maṅgalācaraṇa* of the form of remembering the nature of the Self (*svarūpānusandhānalakṣaṇam*). Thus, he follows the tradition in this regard and sets an example to others, although he himself has no use for such a formality, since he is an incarnation of Lord Śiva. Bhagavān Śaṅkarācārya is the foremost among the cultured (*śiṣṭāgraṇīr Bhagavān Śaṅkarācāryaḥ*); the present work like the others, is for the sake of protecting the good people and the good life (*sādhujana-paripālanārtham*), which is the purpose of an *avatāra* (incarnation). Moreover, being the ideal teacher, he practises what he teaches through precept: and it is thus that he seeks to set others on the road to good life. Hence, at the commencement of this work, he meditates on the supreme Reality by employing the word *sat* (*paramahaṁsaparivrājakācārya-tvād ācāryocita-dharma eva pratīyate*).

Here an objection may be raised. According to Advaita, there is no duality, no world or people to be saved, no teacher or preceptor who could save. Since there is no world apart from one self, what is to be saved, and who is to save? If it be said that we have to postulate an illusory world, and then admit that it is to be saved, such an explanation, says the objector, is not at all intelligible. When it is said that the world is illusory, what is meant is that the world is not (*tasya mithyābhūtasya nāstīty-aparaparyāyatvāt*). Is there any sense in instructing the dream-world? To a man who has woken up from a dream, of what use is the wedding-ceremony performed in the dream?

The reply to this objection is as follows: from the standpoint of the pupil who experiences bondage and seeks to have it removed, the teaching is not meaningless. From this standpoint, the distinctions of God and the world, of preceptor and pupil, caused by nescience, are all quite meaningful. When the wisdom-light dawns, then of course, there is no duality, no world. To such a one, all this is a dream; but not to the unenlightened.

The subject-matter of the present work, as of all works on Vedānta, is Brahman that is now unknown; and the aim or goal is the gaining of Brahman-knowledge (*ajñātaṁ Brāhma viṣayam; jñātaṁ Brāhma prayojanam*).

3

नारीस्तनभरनाभीदेशं
दृष्ट्वा मा गा मोहावेशम् ।
एतन्मांसवसादिविकारं
मनसि विचिन्तय वारं वारम् ॥

nārīstanabharanābhīdeśaṁ
dṛṣṭvā mā gā mohāveśam|
etan-māṁsavasādi-vikāraṁ
manasi vicintaya vāraṁ vāram||

Seeing the seductive female form, do not fall a prey to frenzied delusion. That (female form) is (but) a modification of flesh and fat. Think well thus in your mind again and again.

The cultivation of dispassion (*vairāgya*) is quite essential for one who seeks Self-knowledge. Unless one turns away from the path of pleasure (*preyas*), one cannot gain the good (*śreyas*). In the previous verse, the pursuit of wealth for the sake of wealth was deprecated. In the present one, the disciple is warned against the snares of carnal pleasure. The intention here is not to decry womanhood. Women are not debarred from Vedāntic knowledge.

There have been great *jñānīs* even among women, says Śaṅkara, in his commentary on the *Māṇḍūkya-kārikā*.* What he teaches in the present verse, therefore, is that the passionate desire for the flesh of a woman does great harm to a man. The same would be true of a woman's desire for sensual pleasure. If man and woman consider each other to be but a tool for enjoyment, then each degrades the other.

Carnal desire is compared to an evil spirit, by Svayaṁprakāśa. When one is possessed by it, one ceases to be one self. By incantation this evil spirit should be exorcised; the incantation in this case is discrimination. *taṁ dṛṣṭvā piśāca-grasta iva mohag-rasto mā bhava, vivekamantreṇa uccāṭaya*). "Discriminate and discern that there is no happiness in the objects of enjoyment". The technique of such discrimination is called *pratipakṣa bhāvanā* in the Yoga system. It consists in contemplating the opposite. "If an object fascinates you, look at the opposite side of the object, its ephemeral and unworthy nature, the harm it does, the evil it involves, and extricate yourself from it." Contemplating thus only once may not be enough. One may be deluded again and again on account of the past habits and tendencies. So, one should contemplate again and again till dispassion is generated. "Think in your mind repeatedly of the defective side of the object of pleasure". (*punaḥ punaḥ manasi doṣaṁ cintaya, āvartaya*).

The present verse appears as the sixth verse in Svayaṁprakāśa's text. So, he elaborately discusses the question as to why there should be a discourse on dispassion after *jñāna* has been taught. In *jñāna* also there are grades. In the case of some *jñānīs* there may be lack of dispassion. Some may be active, and may not be free from misery. In the experience of Brahman-bliss there may be grades. In some modes of the mind, the consciousness-aspect of Brahman alone is manifest; in some others, the bliss-aspect too is manifest. And in accordance with the relative purity of the mental modes, there may be differences in the degree of bliss-manifestation. These matters are clearly explained by Vidyāraṇya in his *Pañcadaśī*. Svayaṁprakāśa draws our attention

*See *Readings from Śaṅkara* (Part Two) (Jayanti Series No. 6; Ganesh & Co., Madras, 1961), pp. 134-5.

to this explanation. In short, it is this: dispassion (*vairāgya*), knowledge (*bodha*), and sense-control (*uparama*) are mutually helpful to one another. Mostly they are found together. In some cases, however, they may not be together. Hence, the conclusion of Svayaṁprakāśa is that a discourse on dispassion can never be out of place.

4

नलिनीदलगतजलमतितरलं
तद्वज्जीवितमतिशयचपलम् ।
विद्धि व्याध्यभिमानग्रस्तं
लोकं शोकहतं च समस्तम् ॥

nalinīdalagatajalam atitaralaṁ[1]
tadvaj-jīvitam atiśayacapalam/
viddhi vyādhy-abhimāna-grastaṁ
lokaṁ śokahataṁ ca samastam//

The water on the lotus-leaf is very unsteady; so also is life extremely unstable. Know that the entire world is devoured by disease and conceit, and smitten with sorrow.

Here is *pratipakṣa-bhāvanā* (contemplation of the opposite) in regard to life in general and the world. The first lesson that contemplation on the nature of life yields is that life is fleeting. Life is as unsteady as a particle of water on a lotus-leaf. It is as inconstant as the clouds or as the water kept in a leaky pot (*jaladharapaṭala-bhinnakumbhoda-kavat pratīkṣaṇaṁ vināśi*). Since life is so uncertain, one should not postpone endeavour in the direction of Self-knowledge. Svayaṁprakāśa says: "Leave off the false imagination that life is dependable, and begin early to strive for Self-knowledge. Like a cow which comes to grief by chewing the cud when it ought to graze, do not waste your time and later on repent. Just as a cat does not spare a weeping rat,

1. Svayaṁprakāśa: *jala-lava-taralam.*

so also Death will not leave you, taking pity on you, when the time comes". (*tasmāt cirasthāyīti bhrāntiṁ parityajya ātmajñāne prayatnaṁ śīghram eva kuru. tṛṇasvīkaraṇa-kāle romanthaṁ kurvan paśuriva paścād-anarthaṁ mā bhaja. rudantaṁ mūṣikaṁ mārjāra iva antakas tvāṁ dṛṣṭvā na dayāluḥ bhavet*). So, one must begin even now to pursue the path of Self-knowledge. The Self must be realized here even while living. "If here one knows it", declares the *Kena Upaniṣad*, "then there is truth; and if here one knows it not, great is the destruction" (ii,5.)

Even as life is, the world too is full of misery, and is inconstant. Not only this world, but the other worlds also. Physical disease and mental conceit hold the world in their grip. As the Buddha declared, "All is misery, misery; all is momentary, momentary" (*sarvaṁ duḥkhaṁ duḥkhaṁ sarvaṁ kṣaṇikaṁ kṣaṇikam*). Everything other than Brahman is affected by defects. Even heavenly enjoyment is transitory. So, one should not trust what is finite and perishing; one should make haste to turn one's mind and being towards Brahman.

5

यावद्वित्तोपार्जनसक्त-
स्तावन्निजपरिवारो रक्तः ।
पश्चाज्जीवति जर्जरदेहे
वार्तां कोऽपि न पृच्छति गेहे ॥

yāvad-vittopārjana-saktas-
tāvan-nija-parivāro raktaḥ|
paścāj-jīvati jarjara-dehe
vārtāṁ ko'pi na pṛcchati gehe||

As long as you have the ability to earn money,
so long will your dependents be attached to you.
After that, when you live with an infirm body,
no one would even speak to you a word.

Unfortunately, it is a money-centred world in which we live. An individual is respected and sought after, usually, so long as he has the power of the purse. The dependents attach themselves to the wage-earner and the money-getter in their own self-interest. But as soon as the person on whom they depend is deprived of his economic power, either due to old age or other circumstances, they leave him to his fate. The disabilities of old age are well known. When penury is added to these, life becomes an unbearable burden.

Such a state of things will, however, become a blessing in disguise, if one contemplates its significance and develops dispassion. This will enable one to cease relying on earthly props, and turn to the path of Self-knowledge.

6

यावत्पवनो निवसति देहे
तावत्पृच्छति कुशलं गेहे ।
गतवति वायौ देहापाये
भार्या बिभ्यति तस्मिन्काये ॥

yāvat-pavano nivasati dehe
tāvat-pṛcchati kuśalaṁ gehe|
gatavati vāyau dehāpāye
bhārya bibhyati tasmin kāye||

As long as there is breath in the body, so long do people in the household ask about one's welfare. Once the breath leaves, on the destruction of the body, the dependents dread that very same body.

This, again, is a verse designed to generate dispassion in the mind of the disciple. It is astounding that there is so much of body-worship in the human world. What an amount of time and energy is wasted in the glorification of the body! Turn where one may, one discerns plenty of evidence for the cult of the physical body. But this is a demoniacal cult. In the Upaniṣadic story of Indra-Virocana, Virocana, the chief of the demons, understood Prajāpati as teaching that the body was the self. He attired himself in Sunday clothes, embellished himself with fine ornaments, and looked at his own reflection in a pool of water.

He was mightily pleased, and went back to his kind in order to preach that there was nothing greater than the body.

But let us pause and reflect on the constitution and value of the body. The market value of the average man, according to an American Professor, is about 98c. When the body is dead, not only does it have no value; it becomes a positive disvalue. Even the so-called near and dear ones are afraid to go near the dead body. One should meditate on this phenomenon and become free from attachment to the body.

7

बालस्तावत्क्रीडासक्त-
स्तरुणस्तावत्तरुणीसक्तः ।
वृद्धस्तावच्चिन्तासक्तः
परे ब्रह्मणि कोऽपि न सक्तः ॥

bālastāvat krīḍāsaktas-
taruṇastāvat taruṇīsaktaḥ|
vṛddhastāvac-cintāsaktaḥ
pare[1] brahmaṇi ko'pi na saktaḥ||

When a boy, one is attached to sport; when a youth, one is attached to a young woman; when old, one is attached to anxiety; to the supreme Brahman, no one, alas, is attached!

A man's attachments change from time to time. His obsessions vary in accordance with different periods of life. In his childhood, his preoccupation is with toys and trinkets. He lives in the play-world, and gives himself up to sport. As an adult, he becomes a denizen of the world of romance. Courtship, chivalry, carnal enjoyment occupy his attention. When a man grows old and decrepit, feelings of anxiety, dread, and fear take possession of him. Thus the average individual leads an abnormal life from the start to the finish. He is not himself; he is always something other than himself: his playthings, his family, his worries.

1. Some editions: *parame.*

It is seldom that a man is drawn to the inner Self, Brahman. As the *Kaṭha Upaniṣad* (iv, 1) puts it: "The self-existent God pierced the openings of the senses outward; therefore, one looks outward, not within oneself. But the wise one (rare as such a one is) turns his eye within and beholds the inner Self, desiring immortality". Although such expressions as *attachment* and *desire* are used with reference to the Brahman-Self these do not carry their ordinary meaning. One is not attached to Brahman as one is attached to finite objects. One does not desire Brahman as one desires things. As Sureśvara observes in the *Saṁbandhavārttika*, what is called 'desire for *mokṣa*' is an interest in the eternal Self brought about by discrimination. It is not narrow attachment or blind and unthinking desire.

Verses 5, 6 and 7 do not appear in Svayaṁprakāśa's text.

8

का ते कान्ता कस्ते पुत्रः
संसारोऽयमतीव विचित्रः ।
कस्य त्वं कः कुत आयात-
स्तत्त्वं चिन्तय तदिह भ्रातः ॥

kā te kāntā kaste putraḥ
saṁsāro'yam atīva vicitraḥ |
kasya tvaṁ kaḥ kuta āyātas-
tattvaṁ cintaya tadiha[1] *bhrātaḥ*[2] *||*

Who is your wife? Who is your son? Exceedingly wonderful, indeed, is this empirical process! Of whom are you? Who are you? Whence have you come? O brother, think of that truth here.

Family relations and the institution of the house-hold have only a limited value. They have value insofar as they serve to liberate the individual from ego-centred existence. But when they have served their purpose, they must be left behind. Family

1. Other readings : *tadidam*; *yadidaṁ*.
2. *bhrāntaḥ*; *bhrānta*.

is the home of trial and testing; it is not one's destination. Hence the teacher seeks to instil in the mind of the disciple a sense of detachment. The disciple should outgrow narrow attachments to kindred and clan. This does not mean that he should be cruel to them or hate them; nor even that he should be callous to their interests. What it means is that he should no longer regard them as his property, nor himself as their property. It is those who have a narrow outlook that make a distinction between their own and others. The great ones consider the entire world to be their household.

The present verse teaches a method whereby one may cultivate a sense of detachment. It is the method of discrimination, inquiry. Let one inquire: who is wife, who is son? Wifehood, sonship, etc., are superimpositions. The lady was not wife before marriage. She will cease to be so after sometime. Where was the son before his birth? What happens to him if he dies or is disinherited? When one inquires into the truth, there are no son, etc., in reality (*vicāryamāṇe tattvadṛṣṭyā putrādayo na santi*). Wife, son, etc., appear on account of *māyā* even as the dream wife, son, etc., do. What is called empirical life is a wonder. The world of plurality is an appearance in the non-dual, unconditioned, immutable Self, even as the shape of a vault, blue colour, etc., are appearances in the sky. On inquiry it will be found that no one is no one's kin. (*kāntāputrādayaḥ svapnadṛṣṭa-kāntāputrādivat māyāvaśāt pratīyante saṁsārasya vaicitryaṁ nāma asaṅge advitīye nirvikāre pratīyamānatvāt viyati talamalīnādivat pratītimātram . . . . vicāryamāṇe na kasyāpi kaścid bandhuḥ*).

Let one meditate on the truth about oneself. To whom or to what does one belong ? Whence does one come ? What is one's parentage ? What is one's source ? The empirical being that one identifies oneself with is an appearance occasioned by *māyā*. For the true Self, there is no cause nor source.

Adopting the reading *tadidaṁ* (That is this), Svayaṁprakāśa interprets it as meaning the major text *tat tvam asi* (That thou art). The meaning of the last line, then, would be: Meditate on the truth of the major text "That thou art". The express sense of 'that' is God; the express sense of 'thou' is the individual soul. But the implied sense of both the words is the unconditioned non-dual Self. (*tad-idam-ity-anena tattvamasīti mahāvākyārthaḥ pratipādyate . . . vyaṣṭi-samaṣṭi ajñānadvaya-parityāge kevala-caitanyaṁ tattvamasīti vākyārtho bhavati.*)

9

सत्सङ्गत्वे निस्सङ्गत्वं
निस्सङ्गत्वे निर्मोहत्वम् ।
निर्मोहत्वे निश्चलितत्वं
निश्चलितत्वे जीवन्मुक्तिः ॥

satsaṅgatve nissaṅgatvaṁ
nissaṅgatve nirmohatvam |
nirmohatve niścalitatvaṁ
niścalitatve[1] *jīvanmuktiḥ* ||

Through the company of the good, there arises non-attachment; through non-attachment, there arises freedom from delusion; through delusion-lessness, there arises steadfastness; through steadfastness, there arises liberation in life.

It is the association with the objects of sense that causes evil. The *Bhagavadgītā* (ii, 62-63) vividly describes the links that connect sense-objects with destruction through evil. In a man that contemplates sense-objects, attachment thereto is born; from attachment arises desire; from desire, anger; from anger is born delusion; from delusion, there arises the loss of good memory; from this loss, there comes about the destruction of the intellect; through this, the man perishes. It is the bad company that one keeps that leads him to his doom. The road that takes one to sense-gratification is a stultifying downward path, although it looks attractive at the first sight. To imagine that one would come to good by pursuing this path is as foolish as to think that one would gain immortality by drinking poison (Śaṅkarānanda: *viṣaṁ pibato'maratvamiva asanmārge praviṣṭasya sadgatir na saṁbhavati*).

1. Some editions : *niścalatatve.*

In the present verse, the way out of this impasse is shown. Just as one removes the thorn that has entered into one's flesh with the help of another thorn, one may rid one-self of bad associations through association with the good — good people, good thoughts, good deeds. While association with sense-objects reinforces bondage — the more the association, the stronger the attachment —, association with the good promotes detachment. Since attachment is the parent of delusion, detachment begets the opposite or delusion, viz. wisdom. When one is free from delusion, one becomes steadfast in wisdom (*sthita-prajña*). Such a one is firm in the wisdom of the form 'I am Brahman'. He is free from the three root-desires, viz. desire for son, desire for wealth, and desire for the worlds. He is one who has renounced these. He enjoys in the Self, he sports in the Self (Śaṅkara on the *Gītā*, ii, 54-55: *sthitā pratiṣṭhā aham asmi paraṁ brahma iti prajñā yasya saḥ sthita-prajñaḥ tyaktaputravittalokaiṣaṇaḥ saṁnyāsī ātmārāma ātmakrīḍaḥ sthitaprajñaḥ*). Such a one is a *jīvanmukta* (one liberated while living). The continuance of the body is not a hindrance to *mokṣa*. Śaṅkara observes in his commentary on the *Brahmasūtra*, "How can anyone object to the heart-felt experience of one as possessing Brahman-knowledge even while tenanting a body?" (*kathaṁ hy ekasya sva-hṛdaya-pratyayaṁ brahma-vedanaṁ dehadhāraṇaṁ ca apareṇa pratikṣeptuṁ śakyeta*).

Bhagavān Ramaṇa has rendered this verse into a stanza in Tamil, which is the first in his supplement (*Anubandha*) to *Forty Verses on Existence* (*Uḷḷadu Nāṛpadu*). The following is an English translation :

"By association with the good (the real, the true), attachment to the world will go; when attachment goes, the modification of the mind (with its cause, *māyā*) will be destroyed; those who are free from mental modification are those who are one with the changeless (reality); they are those who have attained release while living (in the body). Cherish their company !"*

**Ramaṇa Maharshi and His Philosophy of Existence. p.* 117.

10

वयसि गते कः कामविकारः
शुष्के नीरे कः कासारः ।
क्षीणे वित्ते कः परिवारो
ज्ञाते तत्त्वे कः संसारः ॥

vayasi gate kaḥ kāmavikāraḥ
śuṣke nīre kaḥ kāsāraḥ |
kṣīṇe vitte kaḥ parivāro
jñāte tattve kaḥ saṁsāraḥ ||

When youth is spent, what lustful play is there? When the water has evaporated, what lake is there? When the money is gone, what dependents are there? When the truth is known, what empirical process is there?

Here are four epigrams to illustrate the truth that when the cause is removed the effect perishes, that when the ground is taken away the consequent cannot stand.

The lustful attitudes go with a youthful body. When youthfulness leaves the body, these attitudes also disappear. It has already been stated that when a youth, one is attached to a young woman (see verse 7).

The next epigram offers an illustration. What constitutes a lake is the water, and not the mere bed or the bund. When there is no water, there is no lake.

What draws dependents to oneself is wealth. When that gets depleted, the dependents will depart (see verse 5).

The cause of the empirical world is nescience. It is ignorance about the truth of the non-dual Self that engenders the perception of plurality and the consequent misery. When the truth is known, then it is seen that there is no plurality at all, no cycle of birth and death.

Verses 9 and 10 do not occur in Svayaṁprakāśa's text.

11

मा कुरु धनजनयौवनगर्वं
हरति निमेषात्कालः सर्वम् ।
मायामयमिदमखिलं हित्वा
ब्रह्मपदं त्वं प्रविश विदित्वा ॥

mā kuru dhanajanayauvanagarvaṁ
harati nimeṣāt kālaḥ sarvam |
māyāmayam idam akhilaṁ hitvā[1]
brahmapadaṁ tvaṁ praviśa viditvā ||

Do not be proud of wealth, kindred, and youth; Time takes away all these in a moment. Leaving aside this entire (world) which is of the nature of an illusion, and knowing the state of Brahman, enter into it.

What bind man to the empirical process are his false conceits born of ignorance. He is deluded into thinking, feeling, and acting in terms of 'my property, my people, my youth', etc., as if these are really his and will save him. These cannot even stand against time, being ephemeral. What is the use of trusting them? Conceit is an obstacle to knowledge; and so one should give it up completely (*abhimānasya jñānapratibandhakatvāt sākalyena taṁ parityaja*). Wealth, kindred, and youth are the tools for sense-enjoyment. But, we have seen that such enjoyment ends only in evil. So, one should not feel proud on account of wealth, etc. Wealth is notorious for its inconstancy. People follow the way of wealth. Youth does not last very long. Who but a fool would cling to them?

This world is an illusory appearance. The following is the inference proving the illusory nature of the world: this world is illusory, because it is an object of experience, like nacre-silver (*idaṁ jagan mithyā, dṛśyatvāt, śuktikārūpyavat*). Hence, one should inquire into the nature of Brahman and realize it. Brahman-

1. Svayaṁprakāśa : *buddhvā*.

nature is not alien to us. It is our own being. We are Brahman (it is not that we have to *become* it), even as Rāghava was Viṣṇu, Karṇa was a son of Kuntī, and the tenth man, in the story of the ten travellers, was not lost in the river-floods.

12

दिनयामिन्यौ सायं प्रातः
शिशिरवसन्तौ पुनरायातः ।
कालः क्रीडति गच्छत्यायु-
स्तदपि न मुञ्चत्याशावायुः ॥

dinayāminyau sāyaṁ prātaḥ
śiśiravasantau punar-āyātaḥ |
kālaḥ krīḍati gacchaty-āyus-
tadapi na muñcaty-āśāvāyuḥ ||

Day and night, dusk and dawn, winter and spring come repeatedly; Time sports, life is fleeting; yet one does not leave the winds of desire.

Days and nights alternate; so do dawns and dusks; the seasons change; the years roll. The wheel of time, whose spokes these are, revolves incessantly and inexorably. With each revolution, life gets shorter; and even the longest life is short. Time plays with life; life is at time's mercy. But man does not realize this and he builds for the future. Not remembering that life is fleeting, he goes on multiplying his desires in the hope of satisfying them. The sense-objects which he desires to possess, after all, are not worth the trouble which he puts himself to in order to gain them. The best of things turn to ashes in his mouth. Like the form of the golden deer which Mārīca took in order to allure Sītā, the objects glitter and look fine in order to drag the unwary man into the quagmire of the world. So, let us be vigilant and resist the temptation of the objects of desire. Let not the winds of desire carry us off our feet. Let us not fall a prey to the vicissitudes of time.

In some editions, the present verse is the last verse of the *Dvādaśamañjarikāstotra*. After this, a verse is added in which the authorship and the occasion for the composition of the hymn are mentioned.

dvādaśamañjarikābhir-aśeṣaḥ
kathito vaiyākaraṇasyaiṣaḥ |
upadeśo'bhūd vidyānipuṇaiḥ
śrīmacchaṁkarabhagavaccaraṇaiḥ ||

At the end of this, there is the following colophon:

iti śrī-guru-śaṅkaravijaye śrīmacchaṅkara-bhagavatpāda-vaiyākaraṇa-saṁvāde paramahaṁsa-pari-vrājakācāryavarya śrīmacchaṅkarācāryopadiṣṭa-dvādaśamañjarikā-stotram.

13

का ते कान्ताधनगतचिन्ता
वातुल किं तव नास्ति नियन्ता ।
त्रिजगति सज्जनसंगतिरेका
भवति भवार्णवतरणे नौका ॥

kā te kāntā-dhana-gata-cintā[1]
vātula kiṁ tava nāsti niyantā |
trijagati sajjana-saṅgatir ekā
bhavati bhavārṇava-taraṇe naukā ||

Why worry about wife, wealth, etc., O crazy one; is there not for you the One who ordains? In the three worlds, it is only the association with good people that can serve as the boat that can carry one across the sea of birth (metempsychosis).

According to some editions, this is the first verse of the *Caturdaśamañjarikā-stotra* said to be the joint composition of fourteen disciples of Śaṅkara.

This particular verse is attributed to Padmapāda.

1. Svayaṁprakāśa : *kāntā-'dhara-gata-cintā.*

According to Svayaṁprakāśa, this is a constituent verse of the *Dvādaśamañjarikā*, and so its author is Śaṅkara. Introducing this verse, he says: Just as one may rouse a man asleep inside a burning house by beating, etc., and enable him to escape, even so the teacher, out of great compassion, again, makes the disciple understand (*pradīptagṛhāntar gāḍha-suptaṁ janaṁ tāḍayitvā calayitvā pādakarādinā prabuddhaṁ bahir-nissārayati yathā paramakāruṇikatvād ācāryās tathā punaḥ bodhayanti*).

Of what avail are anxieties and cares about life, wealth, etc.? According to Svayaṁprakāśa's reading, the meaning would be: why ruminate over the lips of your lady? By meditating on objects of sense, one is only wasting one's time. From the metaphysical standpoint, such meditation is a punishable act. The teacher may well punish his disciple for this. He rebukes the disciple by calling him *vātula*, meaning 'O crest-jewel among fools that constantly think of sense-objects' (*viṣayaparamūḍhaśiromaṇe*), and commands him to desist from this vain and evil meditation.

What is the remedy for this disease? How may one cross the sea of *saṁsāra* (metempsychosis)? One of the potent means is association with the good. Such association is a safe and sure boat which will transport one across the *saṁsāra* — sea. The good and wise ones repeatedly teach the need for cultivating devotion, knowledge, dispassion, etc. They are the great ones who remind us of this need again and again. (*trijagati sajjanānāṁ saṅgatiḥ bhava evārṇavaḥ bhavārṇavaḥ samudraḥ tattāraṇe ekā mukhyā naukā bhavati. bhakti-jñānavairāgyādi punaḥ punaḥ smārayanti bodhayanti ca mahāntaḥ*). Svayaṁprakāśa quotes a verse according to which quiescence (*śama*), inquiry (*vicāra*), contentment (*santoṣa*), and the company of the good (*sādhusamāgama*) are the necessary means for gaining release. (See verse 9).

14

जटिलो मुण्डी लुञ्चितकेशः
काषायाम्बरबहुकृतवेषः ।
पश्यन्नपि च न पश्यति मूढो
ह्युदरनिमित्तं बहुकृतवेषः ॥

jaṭilo[1] *muṇḍī luñcitakeśaḥ*
kāṣāyāmbarabahukṛtaveṣaḥ |
paśyannapi ca na paśyati mūḍho
hyudaranimittaṁ bahukṛtaveṣaḥ ||

The ascetic with matted locks, the one with his head shaven, the one with hairs pulled out one by one, the one who disguises himself variously with the ochre-coloured robes — such a one is a fool who, though seeing, does not see. Indeed, this varied disguise is for the sake of the belly.

This verse is ascribed to Toṭaka.

Here is an indictment of the pseudo-*sannyāsin*, the one who has donned the garb of a *yati* for the purpose of deluding the world. In the case of such a one, the insignia of renunciation do but become a trade-mark. The tonsure of the head, matted locks, yellow robes — these and other features lose their significance if they are adopted for deceiving the people. While it may be the duty of the householder to honour a person if he merely bore the outer marks of renunciation such as the ochre-coloured robes and the monk's staff, the person who receives the honour, if he is not worthy of it, if he is an impostor, will go to perdition. He is like a character in a drama – and that too, a professional who acts the part of a *sannyāsin*. Such a deportment becomes a means for livelihood, even as a factory uniform or military outfit does. Nay, it is much worse. In the case of the other professions, there is correspondence between desert and dress, whereas in the case of the pseudo-*sannyāsin* there is no correlation at all. In the case of the actor-*sannyāsin* in a play, the audience knows that he is not a *sannyāsin* in life. The venom of the pseudo-*sannyāsin* lies in the fact that he passes for a genuine *sannyāsin*. He sees the hollowness of it all; yet he does not want others to see it. The classical example of such a one was Rāvaṇa who assumed the guise of a *sannyāsin* to carry Sītā away to Laṅkā.

1. Vani Vilas edition : *jaṭilī*.

15

अङ्गं गलितं पलितं मुण्डं
दशनविहीनं जातं तुण्डम् ।
वृद्धो याति गृहीत्वा दण्डं
तदपि न मुञ्चत्याशापिण्डम् ।

aṅgaṁ galitaṁ palitaṁ muṇḍaṁ
daśanavihīnaṁ jātaṁ tuṇḍam |
vṛddho yāti gṛhītvā daṇḍaṁ
tadapi na muñcaty-āśāpiṇḍam ||

The body has become decrepit; the head has turned grey; the month has been rendered toothless; grasping a stick, the old man moves about. Even then, the mass of desires does not go.

This verse is ascribed to Hastāmalaka.

The greatest tragedy of life is that the more one grows the more one grabs, that the desires multiply with age. There is almost an inverse ratio between the dilapidation of the body and the filling of the mind with desires. Is it not tragic that when the body has become unfit for sense-enjoyment, the mind should crave for it ? Sense-enjoyment has a double sting; it takes off the edge of the sense organs by making them blunt; it sets the mind afire by making the mind desire for more of the same enjoyment. The mind wants enjoyment, but the body cannot take it. Thus the individual is made to burn at both ends; he is roasted in his own desires. Desires are at the root of man's discomfort and disquiet. They are the sources of misery when they are fulfilled as well as when they are unfulfilled. By his own desires, man is bound.

16

अग्रे वह्निः पृष्ठे भानू
रात्रौ चुबुकसमर्पितजानुः ।
करतलभिक्षस्तरुतलवास-
स्तदपि न मुञ्चत्याशापाशः ॥

agre vahniḥ pṛṣṭhe bhānū
rātrau cubuka-samarpita-jānuḥ |
karatalabhikṣas tarutalavāsa-
stadapi na muñcaty-āśāpāśaḥ ||

In front, there is fire; at the back, there is the sun; in the night, (the ascetic sits) with the knees stuck to the chin; he receives alms in his palms, and lives under the trees; yet the bondage of desire does not leave him.

This verse is ascribed to Subodha.

Verse 14 dealt with the pseudo-*sannyāsin*. The present verse tells us that mere asceticism, even where it is genuine, will not do. We hear, in the Purāṇas, of Rākṣasas who performed severe penances for nefarious purposes. Even otherwise, austerities by themselves will not lead to release. One may starve the senses; but the mind may be extremely passionate. The *Bhagavadgītā* tells us that he is a hypocrite (*mithyācāra*) who merely restrains his organs of action but sits contemplating in his mind the sense-objects (ii,6). Examples of self-denial are not wanting today. Political parties, ideological alignments, scientific and technological pursuits, and training for space-travel — all require a great measure of austerity. But, do they lead to perfection and peace? *Tapasyā* (austerity) may yield power; but this power may be used for gaining either good or bad ends. To avoid bad ends, one must become desireless. Desirelessness is the result of inquiry into the truth; it is the fruit of Self-knowledge.

17

कुरुते गङ्गासागरगमनं
व्रतपरिपालनमथवा दानम् ।
ज्ञानविहीनः सर्वमतेन
मुक्तिं न भजति जन्मशतेन ॥

kurute gaṅgāsāgaragamanaṁ
vrataparipālanam athavā dānam |
jñānavihīnaḥ sarvamatena
muktiṁ na bhajati janmaśatena ||

One goes on a pilgrimage to the place where the Gaṅgā joins the sea;[1] or observes the religious vows with care or offers gifts. But if he be devoid of knowledge, he does not gain release,— according to all schools of thought,— even in a hundred lives.

This verse is ascribed to the Vārttikakāra, i.e. Sureśvara. It is quite pertinent because what is taught in the present verse, viz. that knowledge is the direct means to release, is the central theme of Sureśvara's writings. Here is a verse from the *Saṁbandha-vārttika* (18):

pratyag-yāthātmya-dhīr eva
pratyag-ajñāna-hānikṛt |
sā cā'tmotpattito nānyad-
dhvānta-dhvastāvapekṣate ||

"Knowledge of the true nature of the inner Self alone is the destroyer of the ignorance regarding the inner Self. And, it requires nothing other than its own generation to destroy the darkness (of ignorance)."*

According to Svayaṁprakāśa's text, the present verse is the last verse of the *Dvādaśamañjarikā*; and so, it is a composition of Śaṅkara.

Pilgrimages to holy places such as Kāśī and Rāmeśvaram, religious observances on occasions such as Śrījayantī and Śivarātrī, acts of charity such as digging a tank and building a hospital — these and other pious deeds may purify the mind and make it one-pointed. But, they do not constitute the direct means to release. Except through the knowledge 'I am Brahman,' i.e., except through the knowledge that is the result of inquiry, one does not gain release, even in hundreds of lives. (*ahaṁ brahmāsmīti jñānavihīne vicāra-janyajñāna-rahite puruṣe muktir na saṁbhavet......jñānaṁ vinā ananta-janmabhir vā muktir na bhavati*).

---

1. This may also mean : pilgrimages to Gaṅgā and the ocean, i.e. Kāśī and Rāmeśvaram (Setu).

*See the Madras University edition (1958), p. 10.

Why is it stated that through deeds release cannot be gained? Because deeds are not opposed to ignorance (*kathaṁ karmaṇā muktiḥ na bhaved iti vācyam, ajñānāviruddhatvāt tasya*). As has already been explained, work, worship, etc., effect the cleansing of the mind and the concentration thereof (*karmopāsanādeḥ cittaśuddhiḥ tadekāgrye phalatvāt*). Ignorance, however, is removed only through knowledge. If a stump is mistaken for a thief, and a rope for a snake, these delusions are not destroyed by ringing a bell or by uttering the *Garuḍa-mantra*. As Śaṅkara says (*Gītā-bhāṣya*, iii, 1), "Release results from knowledge alone. This is the conclusive teaching of the *Gītā* and all the Upaniṣads" (*tasmāt kevalād eva jñānān mokṣa iti eṣo'rthaḥ niścito gītāsu sarvopaniṣatsu ca*).

At the end of the present verse which is the twelfth and the last in Svayaṁprakāśa's text, the following *phala-śruti* is added:

dvādaśamañjarikābhiraśeṣaś-
śiṣyāṇāṁ kathito hyupadeśaḥ |
yeṣāṁ naiva karoti vivekaṁ
te pacyante narakam anekam ||

As we have already pointed out in the Introduction, there is no reference here to the grammarian and the grammatical rule.

18

सुरमन्दिरतरुमूलनिवासः
शय्या भूतलमजिनं वासः ।
सर्वपरिग्रहभोगत्यागः
कस्य सुखं न करोति विरागः ॥

suramandiratarumūlanivāsaḥ
śayyā bhūtalam ajinaṁ vāsaḥ |
sarvaparigrahabhogatyāgaḥ
kasya sukhaṁ na karoti virāgaḥ ||

Living in temples or at the foot of trees, sleeping on the ground, wearing deer-skin, renouncing all possessions and their enjoyment—to whom will not dispassion bring happiness?

This verse is ascribed to Nityānanda.

In Svayaṁprakāśa's text, the present verse is the sixth.

In verse 16, we were told that there was no virtue in mere asceticism. What is essential is desirelessness — freedom from passion and attachment. In the present verse, the teaching is that if one is free from desire and attachment, one would naturally avoid all pomp and pleasure. One's life would then be simple and unostentatious. The addition of things only increases one's discomfort. One should travel light. The more one accumulates, the more one has to suffer. If a discriminating person visits a Super-market, he would be astonished to find the endless unnecessary things with which it is stocked. The number of manufactured goods that one can conveniently do without is, indeed, legion. Dependence is always painful. Having become dependent on many things, if even for one day a thing is lacking, one feels miserable. True happiness lies in independence. The really happy person is the one who is free from desires. Happiness comes through giving up (*tyāge sarveṣāṁ sukhaṁ bhavet*).

19

योगरतो वा भोगरतो वा
सङ्गरतो वा सङ्गविहीनः ।
यस्य ब्रह्मणि रमते चित्तं
नन्दति नन्दति नन्दत्येव ॥

yogarato vā bhogarato vā
saṅgarato vā saṅgavihīnaḥ |
yasya brahmaṇi ramate cittaṁ
nandati nandati nandaty-eva ||

Let one practise concentration; or let one indulge in sense-enjoyment. Let one find pleasure in company; or in solitude. He alone is happy, happy, verily happy, whose mind revels in Brahman.

This verse is ascribed to Ānandagiri.

The present verse is a eulogy of the one who has realized Brahman. Concentration or sense-enjoyment makes no difference to him. Society and solitude are the same to him. Standing at Times Square, New York, or living in a Himalayan cave produces no change in him. The reason is that these are not real; only Brahman is.

Certain texts of Scripture say that a *jīvanmukta* may live as he likes, that even such acts as stealing, killing an embryo, etc., do not affect him. These passages should not be interpreted literally. They are meant to be eulogies, and should be understood figuratively. It is not that a *jīvanmukta* would commit crimes. By his very nature, he cannot be a criminal or an immoral person. Only, he is not moral under constraint. He has gone beyond relative good and evil. To his vision, nothing is real other than Brahman. He revels in Brahman; he lives in Brahman; he is Brahman.

20

भगवद्गीता किञ्चिदधीता
गङ्गाजललवकणिका पीता ।
सकृदपि येन मुरारिसमर्चा
क्रियते तस्य यमेन न चर्चा ॥

bhagavadgītā kiñcid-adhītā
gaṅgājalalavakaṇikā pītā |
sakṛd-api yena murāri-samarcā
kriyate tasya yamena na carcā[1] ||

For him, who has studied the *Bhagavadgītā* even a little, who has drunk a drop of the Gaṅgā-water, and who has performed the worship of the Destroyer of the demon Mura (viz. Śrī Kṛṣṇa) at least once, there is no tiff with Yama (the lord of death).

1. Alternative reading : *kurute tasya yamo'pi na carcām.*

This verse is ascribed to Dṛḍhabhakti.

The need for consecrating one's life is stressed here. By leading a consecrated life, one conquers death. The conquest of death means freedom from the fear of death.

The three acts mentioned here are: studying the *Bhagavad-Gītā*, drinking the Gaṅgā-water, and worshipping the Lord.

The *Bhagavad-Gītā* is the teaching which Śrī Kṛṣṇa gave to the world, having made Arjuna the instrument. In the words of Śaṅkara, the *Gītāśāstra* is the essence of the teaching of all the Vedas (*gītā-śāstraṁ samasta-vedārtha-sārasaṅgrahabhūtam*). Because it contains the cream of the Upaniṣads, it is itself called 'Upaniṣad' (Śaṅkarānanda: *gītopaniṣan-nāmnīṁ brahmavidyām*). One of the *dhyāna-ślokas* (meditation-verses) compares the Upaniṣads to cows, Śrī Kṛṣṇa to the milkman, Arjuna to the calf, the *Gītā* to the milk, and the good and wise people to the partakers of the milk. The *Gītā-māhātmya* says that even a little portion of the *Gītā*, if studied with devotion, will lead one to release.

The Gaṅgā water is said to be supremely sacred. The Purāṇas tell us that the heavenly river Gaṅgā was made to descend to the earth by Bhagīratha through *tapas* in order that his dead ancestors might be sanctified. Pious Hindus believe that even a drop of the Gaṅgā water will purify the body and the mind.

The worship of the Lord is the most potent means for overcoming the 'I-am-the-body' idea. The Lord-God is the destroyer of the demon of egoity. If the individual takes refuge in the Lord, no longer will there be the fear of death for him.

21

पुनरपि जननं पुनरपि मरणं
पुनरपि जननीजठरे शयनम् ।
इह संसारे बहुदुस्तारे
कृपयाऽपारे पाहि मुरारे ॥

punarapi jananaṁ punarapi maraṇaṁ
punarapi jananī-jaṭhare śayanam
iha saṁsāre bahu-dustāre
kṛpayā'pāre pāhi murāre||

Repeated birth, repeated death, and repeated lying in mother's womb—this transmigratory process is extensive and difficult to cross: save me, O Destroyer of Mura (O Kṛṣṇa), through your grace!

This verse is ascribed to Nityanātha.

The transmigration of the soul (*jīva*) consists in recurring birth and death, and the consequent travail in the mother's womb before birth and in the world of toil after that. Bhāratī-tīrtha-Vidyāraṇya says in the *Pañcadaśī* that the *jīva* is driven from birth to death and from death to birth in a continuous cycle of empirical existence, like a worm that is dragged in a rushing stream from one whirlpool to another (i, 30), or like the weaver's shuttle that is tosssed back and forth from one side to the other in a loom. Compelled by the force of its own delusion, the *jīva* travels from death to death. The process of *saṁsāra* seems to be perpetual, without beginning or end. It appears to be a shoreless sea. But redemption is possible: the redeemer is God. It is the divine grace that will take the struggling soul safely across the surging waves of *saṃsāra*.

Appealing to Lord Śiva in a verse of the *Śivānandalaharī*, Śaṅkara says: "Me, who am whirling in puerile *saṁsāra* far far away from my goal on account of delusion and lack of discrimination, you must save through your infinite grace. Who can be more deserving of your grace than I? And, who can be a greater refuge to me, in all the three worlds, than you who are the best expert in saving those who are in distress, O Paśupati?"

'Murāri' and 'Paśupati' are the appellations of the same God. He is the destroyer of the demon of ignorance. He is the lord of souls.

22

रथ्याकर्पटविरचितकन्थः
पुण्यापुण्यविवर्जितपन्थः ।
योगी योगनियोजितचित्तो
रमते बालोन्मत्तवदेव ॥

rathyā-karpaṭa-viracita-kanthaḥ
puṇyāpuṇya-vivarjita-panthaḥ[1] |
yogī yoga-niyojita-citto
ramate bālonmattavad-eva ||

He who wears a dress made of rags that lie about in the streets, he who walks in the path that is beyond merit and demerit—the *yogin* whose mind is given up to *yoga* revels (in Brahman) just as a child or as a mad-man.

This verse is ascribed to Yogānanda.

Of the *jīvanmuktas* it is said that they may behave like children, mad men, or ghosts (*bālonmattapiśācavat*). There is no rule for them; they do not live under constraint; they are no longer bound with the chain of cause and effect. They are perfectly free — totally and absolutely free. Their outer appearance may often be misleading. They may be repulsive to look at. They may be utterly foreign to drawing-room manners. Their ways of behaviour may be mysterious and unpredictable. They may not conform to any convention. 'Right' and 'wrong' do not apply to them; 'merit, and 'demerit, do not belong to them. They are beyond the three guṇas of *Prakṛti*; and so, prescriptions and prohibitions have no relevance in their case (*nistraiguṇye pathi vicaratām ko vidhiḥ ko niṣedhaḥ*). They are not victims to the vagaries of the world. They are Brahman-made. They have no bodies. It is the unenlightened that attribute bodies and activities to them.

23

कस्त्वं कोऽहं कुत आयातः
का मे जननी को मे तातः ।
इति परिभावय सर्वमसारं
विश्वं त्यक्त्वा स्वप्नविचारम् ॥

1. Another reading : *panthāḥ*.

kastvaṁ ko'haṁ kuta āyātaḥ
kā me jananī ko me tātaḥ|
iti paribhāvaya sarvam asāraṁ
viśvaṁ tyaktvā svapnavicāram[1]*||*

Who are you? Who am I? Whence have I come? Who is my mother? Who, my father? Thus enquire, leaving aside the entire world which is comparable to a dream, and is essenceless.

This verse is ascribed to Surendra.

The world of waking is non-real like the dream-world, from the metaphysical standpoint. Although from the empirical standpoint there are differences between the waking world and the dream-world, they are, both of them, illusory from the standpoint of the absolute Self. The things that constitute the waking world are the objects of perception, even as the dream-contents are; and what are *perceived* are illusory. In his commentary on the *Māṇḍūkyakārikā* (ii, 4), Śaṅkara puts the argument in the form of a five-membered syllogism: the things seen in waking are illusory (*pratijñā*); because they are seen (*hetu*); like the things seen in dream (*dṛṣṭānta*); as in dream there is illusoriness for the things seen, so even in waking the characteristic of being seen is the same (*hetūpanaya*); therefore, even in waking the illusoriness of things is declared (*nigamana*). Another reason for classing the world of waking with the dream world is that it too is evanescent. What is non-existent in the beginning and at the end, is so even in the present. Ānandagiri gives the following argument: the world of waking is illusory, because it has a beginning and an end, like the dream world, etc.; what has a beginning and an end is illusory, like mirage, etc.[2]

Let one realize the illusory and essenceless nature of the world by asking such questions as: Who am I ? Who are you? Where-

---

1. Alternative reading :
iti paribhāvita-nijasaṁsāraḥ
sarvaṁ tyaktvā svapnavicāraḥ.

2. See the present writer's *Gauḍapāda : A Study in Early Advaita* (*University of Madras*, third edition, 1960), p. 122.

from are we? Who is my mother and who my father? Are the dream-ego and non-ego real? Are the dream-parents real? Are the dream-birth and death facts? Proper inquiry on these lines will reveal the vanity and emptiness of the world.

24

त्वयि मयि चान्यत्रैको विष्णु-
र्व्यर्थं कुप्यसि मय्यसहिष्णुः ।
सर्वस्मिन्नपि पश्यात्मानं
सर्वत्रोत्सृज भेदाज्ञानम् ॥

tvayi mayi cānyatraiko viṣṇur-
vyarthaṁ kupyasi mayyasahiṣṇuḥ/
sarvasminnapi paśyātmānaṁ
sarvatrotsṛja bhedājñānam//

In you, in me, and elsewhere too, there is but one Viṣṇu (God). Vainly do you get angry with me, being impatient. See the Self in all things, and leave off everywhere ignorance which is the cause of difference.

Svayaṁprakāśa combines the first half of the present verse with the second half of the next verse. In his text, this is the eleventh verse.

In some printed editions, this verse (i.e. 24ab+25cd) is ascribed to Medhātithi.

Svayaṁprakāśa introduces this verse in a rather interesting manner. The disciple gets tired of the teacher, and of having to listen to the same instruction over and over again. He develops a sense of disgust, or even a feeling of anger. This is a case of familiarity breeding contempt (*atiparicayād avajñā iti nyāyāt*). The present verse is addressed to such an angry disciple (*kupitaṁ śiṣyaṁ prati kopaśāntim upadiśati*).

If the truth of the omnipresence of the Lord is known who can get angry with whom? One cannot be angry with oneself. One cannot hate oneself. "For the one who sees oneness everywhere", declares a scriptural text, "what delusion is there, and what depression?" It is the one Reality, Viṣṇu, that pervades all beings. In 'you', i.e. in the body of the disciple, in 'me', i.e. in the body of the teacher, and in the bodies of others such as Devadatta, there resides the one Viṣṇu. 'Viṣṇu' means the 'all-pervading' reality. He is the inner ruler, immortal (*tvayi śiṣyaśarīre mayi guruśarīre anyatra devadattaśarīre eko viṣṇur vartate. viṣṇur vyāpakaśīlaḥ. sarvatrāntaryāmirūpeṇa anuvartate.*)

So, the teacher says, see the same Self everywhere; give up ignorance which is the cause of plurality.

25

शत्रौ मित्रे पुत्रे बन्धौ
मा कुरु यत्नं विग्रहसन्धौ ।
भव समचित्तः सर्वत्र त्वं
वाञ्छस्यचिराद्यदि विष्णुत्वम् ॥

śatrau mitre putre bandhau
mā kuru yatnaṁ vigrahasandhau|
bhava samacittaḥ sarvatra tvaṁ
vāñchasyacirād yadi viṣṇutvam||

Make no effort to be either at war with, or in league with, enemy, friend, son, or relative. If you want to attain the status of Viṣṇu (Godhood) soon, be equal-minded towards all things.

In one printed edition, the first half of this verse is combined with the second half of the previous verse; and this is described as *mohamudgara-śeṣa*, i.e. a 'surplus' verse of the *Mohamudgara*.

If there is only one Self, then who is foe and who is friend, who is son and who is a relation? If there is no duality, how can there be unions or partings, friendly meetings or warlike encounters? If anyone is to be regarded as friend or foe at all, then, we must say that self is the friend of self, self is the foe of self (*Gītā*,vi, 5: *ātmaiva hy ātmano bandhuḥ, ātmaiva ripur ātmanaḥ*).

Realizing the sameness (*sama*) or the one Reality everywhere is the final human goal. This is not something which is to be newly accomplished. It is the eternal nature of the Self. It is gained in the sense in which a forgotten ornament round one's neck is said to be gained. Soulhood (*jīvatva*) is illusorily superimposed on Brahman, even as thiefhood is superimposed on a stump. When through realizing the meaning of the major text 'That thou art' the delusion is removed, the self-established Brahman alone remains.

The one who has realized this has an equal-mind, (*samacittaḥ*). This means: (1) To him, friend and foe are the same (*samaṁ śatrumitre viṣaye cittaṁ yasya saḥ samacittaḥ*); (2) he whose mind has taken the form of Brahman which is the plenary unmodified reality (*san nirvikāraṁ brahma pūrṇaṁ samam ity ucyate*); his mind is endowed with the contemplation of the form 'I am always in the plenary reality, Brahman', and thus it attains Brahman (*tadākāraṁ cittaṁ paripūrṇo'smy-ahaṁ sadā iti bhāvanā-vaśāt brahma prāpyate*).

26

कामं क्रोधं लोभं मोहं
त्यक्त्वाऽऽत्मानं भावय कोऽहम् ।
आत्मज्ञानविहीना मूढा-
स्ते पच्यन्ते नरकनिगूढाः ॥

kāmaṁ krodhaṁ lobhaṁ mohaṁ
tyaktvā'tmānaṁ bhāvaya ko'haṁ[1]*|*
ātmajñānavihīnā mūḍhās-
te pacyante narakanigūḍhāḥ||

Leaving off desire, anger, greed, and delusion, make self-inquiry: Who am I? They are fools who are without Self-knowledge: as captives in hell, they are tortured.

---

1. Svayaṁprakāśa : *hitvātmānaṁ paśyata so'ham*; other readings : *paśyati so'ham*; *paśya vimoham.*

This verse is ascribed to Bhāratīvaṁśa.

In Svayaṁprakāśa's text, this is the eighth verse. "Desire, anger, and greed are the thieves resident in the body, ready to carry away the knowledge-gem; so, be vigilant, be vigilant !"

kāmaḥ krodhaś ca lobhaś ca
dehe tiṣṭhanti taskarāḥ|
jñānaratnāpahārāya
tasmāj-jāgrata jāgrata||

'Desire' is the longing for objects. When that longing is obstructed or frustrated, there arises 'anger'. If these two are given up, one becomes eligible for pursuing the path of meditation (*kāmaḥ icchā viṣayeṣu, tasya pratihatau jātā cittavṛttiḥ krodha ity ucyate. tadubhayaparityāge dhyānākārī bhavet*). 'Greed' is the inability to bear the giving up of objects. Erroneous knowledge is 'delusion': it is mistaking the non-real for the real and the real for the non-real (*tyāgāsahiṣṇutā lobhaḥ, viparītabuddhir mohaḥ. atasmiṁs tadbuddhir ity arthaḥ*). One should leave off anger, etc., and engage oneself in Self-inquiry. Let one seek the answer to the question: 'Who am I?'

Bhagavān Ramaṇa puts the essence of Self-inquiry in these words:

nāhaṁ dehaṁ ko'haṁ so'ham

"I am not the body. Who am I ? I am He."

If it be asked, "How can the *jīva* and Brahman be identical ? Surely, the cow cannot be the horse", the reply is: "When the conditioning adjuncts are removed, the consciousness-self is one and the same. Parviscience in the case of the *jīva* and omniscience in the case of Īśvara are adventitious adjuncts. When these are given up, the Self is realized to be non-dual. As in the case of 'This is that Devadatta', or the ether of the pot and the hall, the pure consciousness which is the Self is distinctionless."

Without this knowledge, one is a fool. Such a one suffers in the hell of *saṁsāra*. He is a deceiver of the Self (*ātmavañcaka*) who does not know the real nature of the Self. "The effort required is very small; the fruit is release even here. Yet, men do not wish for the supreme non-duality."

āyāsas tāvad-atyalpaḥ
phalaṁ muktir ihaiva tu|
tathāpi paramādvaitaṁ
naiva vāñchanti mānavāḥ||

27

गेयं गीतानामसहस्रं
ध्येयं श्रीपतिरूपमजस्रम् ।
नेयं सज्जनसङ्गे चित्तं
देयं दीनजनाय च वित्तम् ॥

geyaṁ gītānāmasahasraṁ
dhyeyaṁ śrīpatirūpam ajasram|
neyaṁ sajjana-saṅge cittaṁ[1]
deyaṁ dīnajanāya ca vittam||

The *Bhagavadgītā* and the *Sahasranāma* should be sung; the form of the Lord of Lakṣmī (Viṣṇu) should be always meditated on; the mind should be led to the company of the good; and wealth should be distributed among the indigent.

This verse is ascribed to Sumati, the last of the fourteen disciples.

A four-fold discipline is recommended here: (1) study of the sacred texts; (2) meditation on the holy form of the Lord; (3) association with the good; and (4) sharing of what one has with those people who are in need.

According to some editions, this is the last verse of the *Caturdaśamañjarikāstotra.* The following verse is added here, wherein are mentioned the authorship and occasion:

1. Alternative reading :
neyaṁ sajjana-saṅgatim aniśam.

mūḍhaḥ kaścana vaiyākaraṇo
ḍukṛñkaraṇādhyayana-dhurīṇaḥ|
śrīmacchaṅkarabhagavacchiṣyair
bodhita āsīcchoditakaraṇaḥ||

This is followed by the colophon:

iti śrī-guru - śaṅkaravijaye śrīmacchaṅkara - bhagavatpāda-vaiyākaraṇa - saṁvāde paramahaṁsa - parivrājakācāryavarya śrīmac - chaṅkarācāryājñaptaśiṣyopanyasta - caturdaśamañjarikā-stotram.

28

सुखतः क्रियते रामाभोगः
पश्चाद्धन्त शरीरे रोगः ।
यद्यपि लोके मरणं शरणं
तदपि न मुञ्चति पापाचरणम् ॥

sukhataḥ kriyate rāmābhogaḥ
paścāddhanta śarīre rogaḥ |
yadyapi loke maraṇaṁ śaraṇaṁ
tadapi na muñcati pāpācaraṇam ||

One easily takes to carnal enjoyment; afterwards, lo, there is disease of the body. Although, in the world, death is the refuge, even then one does not relinquish sinful ways.

The pleasure of the lowest type (*tāmasasukha*), according to the *Bhagavad-gītā*, is that which is enjoyable at the beginning but very painful in the end. Sense-indulgence inevitably results in unpleasant consequences to the body and mind.

One knows that a particular course of action is sinful. Yet, one does not avoid it. One knows that death is inevitable. Yet, one does not keep oneself away from wrongful deeds. Such is the play of *māyā* !

29

अर्थमनर्थं भावय नित्यं
नास्ति ततः सुखलेशः सत्यम् ।
पुत्रादपि धनभाजां भीतिः
सर्वत्रैषा विहिता रीतिः ॥

artham anarthaṁ bhāvaya nityaṁ
nāsti tataḥ sukhaleśaḥ satyam|
putrādapi dhanabhājāṁ bhītiḥ
sarvatraiṣā vihitā rītiḥ||

Wealth is no good: thus reflect always; there is not the least happiness therefrom: this is the truth. For the wealthy, there is fear even from a son: everywhere this is the regular mode.

This is the second verse in Svayaṁprakāśa's text.

The evil nature of wealth has already been explained. The present verse confirms it by saying that on account of property even one's own son, etc., may become inimical.

30

प्राणायामं प्रत्याहारं
नित्यानित्यविवेकविचारम् ।
जाप्यसमेतसमाधिविधानं
कुर्ववधानं महदवधानम् ॥

prāṇāyāmaṁ pratyāhāraṁ
nityānityavivekavicāram|
jāpyasametasamādhividhānaṁ
kurvavadhānaṁ mahadavadhānaṁ||

The regulation of breath, the withdrawal of the senses (from their respective objects), the inquiry consisting in the discrimination between the eternal and the non-eternal, the method of mind-control associated with the muttering of *mantras* — perform these with great care.

In order to gain eligibility for Self-knowledge, one should practise *yoga* along with inquiry. The control of breath, the withdrawal of the senses from their respective objects, the repetition of the sacred *mantra*, the concentration of mind, the discrimination of the eternal from the non-eternal — these should be performed with devotion and faith.

For the place of *Yoga* in Vedānta, see the chapter 'Dhyāna-dīpa' in the *Pañcadaśī*.

31

गुरुचरणाम्बुजनिर्भरभक्तः
संसारादचिराद्भव मुक्तः ।
सेन्द्रियमानसनियमादेवं
द्रक्ष्यसि निजहृदयस्थं देवम् ॥

gurucaraṇāmbuja-nirbhara-bhaktaḥ
saṁsārād-acirād-bhava muktaḥ|
sendriya-mānasa-niyamād-evaṁ[1]
drakṣyasi nijahṛdayasthaṁ devam||

Being devoted completely to the lotus-feet of the Master, become released soon from the transmigratory process. Thus, through the discipline of sense and mind-control, you will behold the Deity that resides in your heart.

This is the concluding verse according to the text adopted here. In this verse, the need for devotion to the *Guru* is stressed. It may be noted that *Govinda* was the name of Śaṅkara's *Guru*.

Even in the matter of acquiring secular knowledge, it is well known that a preceptor is indispensable. Need it then be said that the instruction of a preceptor is quite essential for one

1. Vani Vilas edition : *niyamād-eva*.

to gain sacred knowledge? *The Chāndogya Upaniṣad* declares that he who has a preceptor knows the Self (*ācāryavān puruṣo veda*, vi, xiv, 2), and gives the analogy of a citizen of Gāndhāra who when left in a strange uninhabited country blindfolded, gets his bandage loosened with the help of a gentleman who tells him 'Gāndhāra lies in this direction', asks his way from village to village, and finally arrives at his destination. And, the Upaniṣad asserts emphatically that it is only such knowledge as is learnt from the preceptor that is the best *ācāryāddhaiva vidyā viditā sādhiṣṭhaṁ prāpati*, iv, ix 3). The *Muṇḍaka Upaniṣad* teaches that for the sake of the highest knowledge, one should go, fuel in hand, to a preceptor (*guru*) who is learned in the scriptures and established in Brahman (I, ii, 12). Commenting on this text, Śaṅkara says, "Even a well-read person should not aim at gaining Brahman-knowledge independently" (*śāstrajño'pi svātantryeṇa brahmajñānānveṣaṇaṁ na kuryāt*). In fact, no difference should be made, the *śāstras* tell us, between God and the preceptor. The *Śvetāśvatara Upaniṣad* ends with this note: "These matters which have been declared become manifest to one who has the highest devotion for God, and for the preceptor even as for God." According to another interpretation: "Even matters that have not been declared (in the Upaniṣad) become manifest to such a one."

And so, in the last verse of *Bhaja Govindam*, devotion for *guru* is stressed. He who has this devotion attains release in no time. What does the *guru* teach? The quintessence of his teaching to his disciple is: "Control your senses and mind: inquire and discriminate: and you will behold the Supreme Reality that resides in your Heart."

IV

ŚIVĀNANDALAHARĪ

INTRODUCTION

The *Śivānandalaharī*, ascribed by tradition to Ādi Śaṅkara, is a grand hymn to Śiva, beautiful in form and content. In the ninty-eighth verse, the excellences of this composition are mentioned by the author himself, without the least exaggeration. Employing words in a double sense, (*śleṣa*), which itself is a skilled poetic device, the poem is offered to the Lord for His pleasure; He is invited to take this ideal maiden endowed with all the graces as His bride. The graces that adorn the poem cover both style and sense. The lilting cadences and divine music of the words will enthrall the reader's heart; the profound truths expressed in those words will exalt his mind. Out of great compassion for the struggling souls, Śrī Śaṅkara has given in this century of verses a litany that can serve as a constant and unfailing guide in their march towards perfection.

As the *Śivānandalaharī* is a hymn to Śiva, the greatness of God as Śiva is stressed in every verse. The stories and legends of Śiva that are to be found in the Purāṇas are made use of to illustrate the benignant and benevolent nature of Śiva. Some Vedic scholars are of the view that Rudra is a malevolent deity intent on destroying those whom he dislikes, and that he came to be called 'Śiva' euphemistically later on. One writer contrasts Rudra-Śiva, whom he regards as the god that is feared, with

Viṣṇu-Nārāyaṇa who is the god that is loved. That there is no basis for such a view will be evident to those who study the texts in their proper context. The picture of Śiva that we have in the *Śivānandalaharī* is that of the supreme God who is the source of auspiciousness (*Śaṁbhu*), who does what is auspicious (*Śaṅkara*), who is auspiciousness itself (*Śiva*). Śiva is the saviour of souls, the giver of all that is good. His grace confers on the soul the highest good, *mokṣa*.

The central theme of the *Śivānandalaharī* is devotion to God. In this poem, Ācārya Śaṅkara makes use of every literary device to set forth the nature of devotion (*bhakti*) and to indicate its importance in the scheme of spiritual discipline. Devotion means 'directing the modes of the mind to flow constantly towards God and making them get absorbed there.' Thinking, feeling, and willing are the main functions of the mind. When these functions come to have God alone as their end, the mind is said to be devoted. In the course of teaching this profound truth, Śaṅkara compares the mind to several things and uses picturesque language. Lessons are drawn from inanimate things and animate beings, and from every grade of existence, sub-human, human, and divine. Various expressions are used to refer to the cognitive aspect of mind: *citta*, *cetas*, *buddhi*, and *manas*; the word *hṛdaya* which is also used implies the emotional side of mind.; and *dhṛti* indicates resolve and the strength of will. Different comparisons are given to show that each one of these functions should be dedicated to Śiva.

Seeking to define devotion in a verse (61), Śaṅkara compares the constant flow of the mind towards God (a) to the movement of the seeds of the *aṅkola* tree, on falling to the ground, towards the trunk of the tree and sticking there, (b) to the attraction of iron-filings to the magnet, (c) to the unceasing attachment of a chaste woman to her lord, (d) to the entwining of a creeper around a tree, and (e) to the coursing of a river to the ocean. The point in all these comparisons is the constancy of attachment, the singleness of purpose. The lower member in each of these analogies cannot but be united with the higher member. When the mind is united with God in a similar manner, we have devotion.

The mind of the devotee knows no other end except the Lord.

The longing of the devoted mind for God is compared to the longing of the swan for the lotus-tank, of the *cātaka* bird for the dark rain-cloud, of the *cakravāka* bird for the sun, and of the *cakora* bird for the moon (59). Here the mind filled with devotion is compared to four species of birds. Each of these birds longs for what sustains them: the swan lives by eating lotus-stalks; the *cātaka* can drink only the rain-drops from the clouds; the *cakravāka* looks forward eagerly to sun-rise; and the *cakora* is sustained by lunar rays. So also, the devoted mind finds solace only in God; nothing else can satisfy it.

The mind of the worldling does not easily turn towards God. Like a monkey, it leaps from desire to desire. But if Śiva who plays the role of a mendicant will bind the monkey with the cord of devotion, then it will do His bidding and thus be an aid to Him (20). The mind is like a thief; it wants to grab and amass wealth even by illegitimate means; passions like greed and avarice hold it in their power; it is driven to act in violation of *dharma*. Who can control this thief except the Arch-thief who is Śiva? It is He that must come to our rescue and save us by keeping this mind-thief under effective check (22). The mind is mighty and turbulent like an untamed elephant. Like an elephant in the period of heat, it roams about in all directions, and in a wild manner. It is Śiva that should bind it tactfully with the cord of devotion, using the goad of courage and the machinery of intelligence, and tie it to the peg of His Feet, so that it may not stray (96, 97). The mind is like a dense forest which is the abode of wild beasts. The passions are the beasts. Śiva who is the Primeval Hunter will find in this forest plenty of game. Let Him engage Himself in sport and derive delight therefrom (43). The mind is an old box filled with disagreeable odours in the form of residual impressions. If these odours are to be overpowered and removed, Śiva must fill the box with the pleasant scents of divinity. By His Grace, let Him remove from the mind desire, delusion, and passion (74).

What one should offer to God is one's own mind and heart. Why should a devotee put himself to the trouble of gathering external flowers? Why go to the forests, hills and tanks in quest of blooms? The heart-lotus is the most acceptable offering to the Lord (9). It is only when the heart-lotus is offered to the

Lord that He takes on Himself all the burdens of the devotee (11). Let us invite the honey-bee, the Lord, to revel in the mind-lotus (61). Let the Lord occupy the tent of the mind, which has firm resolve as the central pole, which is tied with the ropes of constant qualities, which can be moved at will, which is beautiful and finely decorated, and which is pure and spotlessly clean (21). Why should the Lord still use His conventional mount, the Bull? He is the leader of all the worlds. Let Him ride the mind-horse which is endowed with all the excellences (75). Śiva has to perform very hard tasks with His Feet — tasks such as kicking at the chest of Yama (Death), destroying the stiff Apasmāra (Nescience), walking on Mount Kailāśa, and rubbing against the crowns worn by the gods on their heads. How can He undertake these operations with bare feet? Let Him wear the jewelled footwear of the mind which will stand all the rough usage (64). Śiva likes to reside in fortresses. Let Him stay, then, in the mind-fortress which is impregnable, well-guarded, and provided with every convenience (42). If only Śiva the Lion, will come into the mind-cave and remain there, there will be no fear from any quarter (40). If in the capital-city of the mind-lotus the King of kings takes His seat, all will be well: virtue will flourish, sins will disappear, passions will be banished, the Golden Age will dawn, and there will be all-round prosperity (39). If Śiva, the Moon, appears in the mind-sky, the waves of the ocean of bliss will leap, and all good people will rejoice (38). Let us perform the auspicious *puṇyāhavācana*, making the mind the pot, filling it with the ambrosia of joy, placing thereon the tender leaves of the Feet of the Lord and the cocoanut of wisdom, and uttering the sacred formula of the Lord's name (36).

The mind is a maiden fit to serve the Lord. She has all the qualifications required for such service. Let her be accepted as a companion to Gaurī in the Lord's service (84). Like a woman separated from her lord, the mind constantly thinks of Śiva and is lost in contemplation. The name of Śiva works like a magic-spell on her. All her faculties have only one concern, and that is Śiva (77). Let Śiva hasten and take care of the mind-bride. It is His duty to instruct and train her. She deserves to have Him as her Lord, for she knows how to serve, is humble, has a good heart, and is devoted to the pursuit of goodness (78).

Devotion has to be cultivated with infinite care and patience. The farm of the heart should be irrigated with the ambrosial waters of the story of Śiva brought with the help of the intellect as water-wheel through the channels of poesy; then, in that farm will arise a goodly crop, and there will be no fear of a famine (40). The heart is a garden, and meditation, is the spring season. The garden in this season is full of creeper-plants of devotion, which having shed the old leaves of sin have taken on fresh tender leaves of merit. The words that repeat the sacred name are the blooms, bearing sweet scents in the form of good impressions. Wisdom and bliss are the full-blown flowers, filled with the honey of immortality. The fruit that the creepers of devotion bear is the supreme consciousness (47). The mind serves as a *pandal* for the creeper of devotion to spread and bear fruit (49). The mind is like a lake; if it is filled with the waters of joy that come down from the cloud of devotion, then life will come to fruition, and not otherwise (76). The flood of Śiva-bliss flows from the river of the story of Śiva, removes the dust of sin, courses through the channels of the intellect, destroys the sorrow caused by transmigration, and fills the lake-land of the mind (2).

In a few verses, Śaṅkara pictures the mind as a swan, and exhorts it to seek refuge in the Feet of the Lord. The Lord's Feet are like a mansion, brilliantly lit by the splendour of their toe-nails, white-washed with the rays of the waxing moon, and embellished with rubies. Let the royal swan, the mind, resort to this mansion (46). The mind-bird should rest in the nest of the Feet of the Lord, forsaking all futile wanderings. Here, it will find contentment and felicity, and will be freed from weariness and sorrow (45). Mind, the best of swans — let it betake itself to the lake of Śiva-meditation which is the reservoir of eternal bliss, wherein bloom the lotus-hearts of gods and sages; let not the mind-swan wander in the muddy pools of service to those that are low (48).

Advaita-experience is the final goal of devotion to, and meditation on, Śiva. An approach to Advaita may be made through any form of *saguṇa*-worship, or through any mode of metaphysics. Ācārya Śaṅkara adopts in the *Śivānandalaharī* the Śaiva path for leading the devotee to Brahman-realization. Realization is gained when the bonds of *saṁsāra* break. The bonds will break when nescience, is destroyed. For the destruction of nescience, one should have wisdom. Wisdom dawns through the grace of God. It is wrong to think that there is no place for God or for devotion in Advaita. As a well-known verse puts it:

īśvarānugrahād eva puṁsām advaita-vāsanā|
mahadbhaya-paritrāṇā dvitrāṇām upajāyate||

'It is by God's grace alone that an inclination towards Advaita comes to men — to two or three — that will save them from great fear (viz., *saṁsāra*).'

Bhagavān Śrī Ramaṇa has given us a selection from the *Śivānandalaharī*, consisting of ten verses rearranged, for the sake of conveying the quintessence of the poem. He has composed a mnemonic verse indicating the initial letters of the verses selected and their order in the selection:

aṁ-bhak jana-ghaṭo-vakṣaḥ
nara-guhā-gabhī-vaṭuḥ|
ādyā-daśa śivānanda-
laharī-śloka-sūcikā||

The ten verses are: 61, 76, 83, 6, 65, 10, 12, 9, 11 and 91 (61) A definition of devotion is given with apt analogies. Devotion is constant contemplation of God. (76) When devotion fills the mind, life becomes worth-while and fruitful. (83) There is no point in being devoted to what is finite and limited; the object of true devotion is the Infinite Reality, God (6) Logic cannot be a substitute for devotion. Skill in the art of argumentation will not yield happiness. It will only result in a weariness of the mind. (65) The devotee meets with no such bitterness. He gains the supreme happiness, conquering death. Even the gods adore him. (10) What is important is devotion. Other considerations and conditions of life are of no consequence. (12) One may live anywhere and follow any mode of discipline; true *yoga* is devotion to God. (9) Devotion does not consist in mere external offering of flowers, etc., to God; it is the heart-gift that is true devotion. (11) One may be a devotee in any stage of life; if one surrenders oneself to God, He is ready to take on all the burdens. (91) The end of devotion is *mokṣa*. Devotion to God removes the darkness of ignorance by shedding the light of wisdom.

ŚIVĀNANDALAHARĪ

शिवानन्दलहरी

1

कलाभ्यां चूडालंकृतशशिकलाभ्यां निजतपः-
फलाभ्यां भक्तेषु प्रकटितफलाभ्यां भवतु मे ।
शिवाभ्यामस्तोकत्रिभुवनशिवाभ्यां हृदि पुन-
र्भवाभ्यामानन्दस्फुरदनुभवाभ्यां नतिरियम् ॥

kalābhyāṁ cūḍālaṁkṛta-śaśikalābhyāṁ nijatapaḥ-
phalābhyāṁ bhakteṣu prakaṭita-phalābhyāṁ bhavatu me|
śivābhyām astoka-tribhuvana-śivābhyāṁ hṛdi punar-
bhavābhyām ānandasphurad-anubhavābhyāṁ natiriyam||

May this my obeisance be to the two Auspicious Ones (Śiva and Pārvatī), who constitute the essence of all learning, who wear on the head the crescent-moon as embellishment, who are, each to the other, the fruit of their own respective penances, who confer benefits on the devotees, who make all the three worlds blessed, who appear repeatedly in the heart, and who engender the experience of manifest happiness!

In this invocatory verse, obeisance is offered to Pārvatī and Parameśvara, the first parents of the world. In truth, they are not different from each other; they are aspects of the same reality. The *ardhanārīśvara* (half male—half female) form of the Lord has a deep significance. *Māyā* has no locus apart from Brahman. *Prakṛti* cannot be separated from *Īśvara*. As Kālidāsa puts it, Pārvatī and Parameśvara are inseparable even as word and meaning are (*vāgarthāviva saṁpṛktau*). Whatever is true of the one is true of the other. The attributes and adornments of the one belong to the other also. For instance, the crescent moon adorns both Pārvatī and Parameśvara. They are both of them the source of culture and the arts. They become manifest together in the devotee's heart.

The supreme Reality has no gender; and all the three genders belong to it. The term *Śiva*, meaning the auspicious, may be expressed in any of the genders: *Śivaḥ* (m), *Śivā* (f), and *Śivam* (n). Here, in this invocatory verse, Ācārya Śaṅkara adopts the form *Śivaḥ-Śivā* in the dual number (*Śivābhyāṁ*).

2

गलन्ती शंभो त्वच्चरितसरितः किल्बिषरजो
दलन्ती धीकुल्यासरणिषु पतन्ती विजयताम् ।
दिशन्ती संसारभ्रमणपरितापोपशमनं
वसन्ती मच्चेतोह्रदभुवि शिवानन्दलहरी ॥

galantī śaṁbho tvaccaritasaritaḥ kilbiṣarajo
dalantī dhīkulyāsaraṇiṣu patantī vijayatām/
diśantī saṁsāra-bhramaṇa-paritāpopa-śamanaṁ
vasantī maccetohradabhuvi śivānandalaharī//

O Śaṁbhu! Victory be to the Flood of Śiva-Bliss, which flows from the river of Thy story, removes the dust of sin, courses through the channels of the intellect, yields the destruction of sorrow caused by wandering in *saṁsāra*, and remains in the lake-land of my mind !

The present Hymn bears the title *Śivānandalaharī* which means 'the Flood of Śiva-Bliss'. Śiva the supreme Reality is Bliss. It is with the Bliss that is Śiva that the mind must be filled. How should the mind be filled ? The magnificent story of Śiva is the water. It should be brought to the mind through the channel of the intellect. Even as it starts flowing, it removes the dust of sin. And, the supreme fruit it yields is release from bondage.

Those who listen to the *Śivānandalaharī* and are moved by it will overcome sin and sorrow and gain the final human goal which is release.

3

त्रयीवेद्यं हृद्यं त्रिपुरहरमाद्यं त्रिनयनं
जटाभारोदारं चलदुरगहारं मृगधरम् ।
महादेवं देवं मयि सदयभावं पशुपतिं
चिदालम्बं साम्बं शिवमतिविडम्बं हृदि भजे ॥

trayīvedyaṁ hṛdyaṁ tripuraharam ādyaṁ trinayanaṁ
jaṭābhārodāraṁ caladuragahāraṁ mṛgadharam|
mahādevaṁ devaṁ mayi sadayabhāvaṁ paśupatiṁ
cidālambaṁ sāmbaṁ śivam ativiḍambaṁ hṛdi bhaje||

In my heart do I worship Śiva who is knowable through the three Vedas, who is delightful to the heart, who destroyed the three Cities, who is primeval and has three eyes, who looks majestic with a profusion of matted locks, who wears the wriggling snakes as ornaments and bears an antelope, who is the great God, the Divinity, who is gracious to me, who is the lord of souls, and the basic consciousness, who is in the company of His Spouse, and who enacts the ways of the world.

Here are set forth some of the characteristics of Śiva. He is *mahādeva*, the supreme deity, the shining lord (*deva*). He is the source of the scriptures; He is to be known through the scriptures (*trayīvedya*). He is the origin of all things, their first cause (*ādya*).

He is the destroyer of the three cities or castles made of iron, silver and gold. The following is the story relating to this: According to *Mahābhārata*, Tāraka, the demon, was killed by Kārttikeya. The demon's three sons Tārakākṣa, Kamalākṣa, and Vidyunmālī, performed penances and obtained from Brahmā the power to occupy three castles which could move at their behests. It was only after a thousand years that they could be destroyed with a single arrow. The three demons became very powerful and harassed the gods and the good people. At last, the gods went to Śiva and prayed that He should save them. Śiva gained one half of the strength of all the gods, and thus became *mahādeva*. With Viṣṇu as the arrow, Agni as its barb, Yama as its feather, the Veda as the bow, Savitṛ as the bowstring, and Brahmā as the charioteer, Śiva destroyed the three cities. Hence He is called *tripurahara*, *tripurāri*, *purahara*, *hara*. Symbolically, the three cities signify the three bodies, the causal (*kāraṇa*), the subtle (*sūkṣma*), and the gross (*sthūla*), that bind the soul. It is through the grace of Śiva that these bodies are destroyed and the soul gains release.

Śiva has three eyes (*trinayana*), the natural two and the third in the middle of the forehead. There is a legend regarding the appearance of the third eye. Pārvatī in a playful mood closed the normal eyes of her Lord with her hands. At once, the entire world became enshrouded in darkness. Out of compassion for the world, the Lord created for Himself the third eye in His forehead. Symbolically, the three eyes stand for the three lights of the world, viz., the sun, the moon, and fire.

Śiva wears a profusion of matted locks (*jaṭābhāra*)—a sign of the ascetic ideal. When He dances, the hair spreads out in eight parts representing the eight cardinal points.

Among other things, serpents adorn Śiva's body, and deer stands on one of His hands. The ṛṣis of Dārukavana once performed a sacrifice with a view to quell Śiva. Among the dreadful objects that issued out of the sacrifice were serpents and a deer. But these could do nothing as against Śiva. He wore the serpents as ornaments and bore the deer in one of His hands.

For *cidālambaṁ*, there is an alternative reading: *cidānandaṁ*, meaning 'consciousness-bliss'.

4

सहस्रं वर्तन्ते जगति विबुधाः क्षुद्रफलदा
न मन्ये स्वप्ने वा तदनुसरणं तत्कृतफलम् ।

हरिब्रह्मादीनामपि निकटभाजामसुलभं
चिरं याचे शंभो शिव तव पदाम्भोजभजनम् ।।

sahasraṁ vartante jagati vibudhāḥ kṣudraphaladā
na manye svapne vā tadanusaraṇaṁ tatkṛtaphalam|
haribrahmādīnām api nikaṭabhājām asulabhaṁ
ciraṁ yāce śaṁbho śiva tava padāmbhojabhajanam||

Thousands of gods there are in the world who grant puerile benefits; even in my dreams I do not think of following them or of the benefits granted by them. O Śambhu ! O Śiva ! What I have been for a long time asking for is the worship of Thy lotus-feet, which does not come easily even to those that are near Thee, such as Viṣṇu and Brahmā.

Śiva is the supreme Reality. Gaining Him should be the goal of life. Anything short of this ideal will only make one continue to revolve in the cycle of bondage. Nothing but the saving Feet of the Lord will save the soul from *saṁsāra.* The gods and godlings — there are so many of them — may give worldly success and even heavenly enjoyment. But these, after all, have little value for one who seeks the final beatitude.

Compare Yāmunācārya's *Stotra-ratna*, verse 27.

tavāmṛtasyandini pādapaṅkaje
niveśitātmā katham anyadicchati|
sthite'ravinde makarandanirbhare
madhuvrato nekṣurakaṁ hi vīkṣate||

"The soul which has entered Thy lotus-feet shedding nectar — how can it ever desire anything else ? When there is the lotus laden with honey, the bee, indeed, does not even cast a glance at the *ikṣuraka* flower (which is without fragrance or honey)."

5

स्मृतौ शास्त्रे वैद्ये शकुनकवितागानफणितौ
पुराणे मन्त्रे वा स्तुतिनटनहास्येष्ववचतुरः ।

कथं राज्ञां प्रीतिर्भवति मयि कोऽहं पशुपते
पशुं मां सर्वज्ञ प्रथितकृपया पालय विभो ॥

smṛtau śāstre vaidye śakuna-kavitā-gānaphaṇitau
purāṇe mantre vā stuti-naṭana-hāsyeṣvacaturaḥ/
kathaṁ rājñāṁ prītir bhavati mayi ko'haṁ paśupate
paśuṁ māṁ sarvajña prathita-kṛpayā pālaya vibho//

I am not learned in the Traditional Codes, or in the philosophical texts, in the art of medicine, or in the articulation of the science of portents, poesy or music, or in the ancient lore, or in the technique of mystic formulas, or in the arts of praising, dancing and humouring. How then, will the kings be pleased with me ? O Lord of souls, the omniscient and renowned One! O the all-pervading Lord! Save me, who am a soul, through Thy Grace!

For worldly success, one should seek to please those who are in power. In order to please them, one should gain mastery over the secular arts and the sacred lore. But this is not necessary and is of no use in the matter of deserving the grace of God. What one has to do is to surrender oneself to Him.

6

घटो वा मृत्पिण्डोऽप्यणुरपि च धूमोऽग्निरचलः
पटो वा तन्तुर्वा परिहरति किं घोरशमनम् ।
वृथा कण्ठक्षोभं वहसि तरसा तर्कवचसा
पदाम्भोजं शंभोर्भज परमसौख्यं व्रज सुधीः ।

ghaṭo vā mṛtpiṇḍo'py aṇurapi ca dhūmo 'gniracalaḥ
paṭo vā tanturvā pariharati kiṁ ghoraśamanam/
vṛthā kaṇṭhakṣobhaṁ vahasi tarasā tarkavacasā
padāmbhojaṁ śambhorbhaja paramasaukhyaṁ vraja sudhīḥ//

Whether it be pot or lump of clay, or atom, whether it be smoke, fire, or mountain, whether it be cloth or thread — will any of these serve as a remedy for horrible death! You are only straining your throat unnecessarily by logic-chopping! O wise one, hasten to worship the lotus-feet of Śaṁbhu, and attain the supreme happiness.

Of what value is secular logic? You may argue for argument's sake, and silence your adversary through a show of intellectual might. But in what manner will that do you good? The forms of reasoning and the theories of causation will not bring you enlightenment. He who is wise will not waste his time in vain disputation and logic-chopping. He will seek refuge at the lotus-feet of the Lord of souls.

7

मनस्ते पादाब्जे निवसतु वचः स्तोत्रफणितौ
करौ चाभ्यर्चायां श्रुतिरपि कथाकर्णनविधौ ।
तव ध्याने बुद्धिर्नयनयुगलं मूर्तिविभवे
परग्रन्थान्कैर्वा परमशिव जाने परमतः ॥

manaste pādābje nivasatu vacaḥ stotra-phaṇitau
karau cābhyarcāyāṁ śrutirapi kathākarṇanavidhau/
tava dhyāne buddhir nayanayugalaṁ mūrtivibhave
paragranthān kairvā pramaśiva jāne param ataḥ//

O the supreme Śiva! Let my mind stay at Thy lotus-feet; let my speech be engaged in uttering Thy praise; my hands in Thy worship; my sense of hearing in listening to Thy story; my intellect in meditation on Thee; and my eyes in looking at Thy splendid form! This being so, through which other sense-organs will I learn other texts?

How should one seek the Lord's protection? With all one's faculties of sense, mind and heart. The technique of devotion consists in concentrating one's attention on God. When a man is in love with a person, how does he behave? He is drawn entirely towards that person without any reservation; his actions, speech and mind come to have only one end, which is to please his object of love. Similarly, the devotee should dedicate his entire being to God. God should become the sole object of his sense-functions and mental modes. All the devotee's interests are thus centred in God. God becomes his one occupation. How will he then attend to anything else? Of what use are the "texts" to him? For, he has gained the purpose of all learning.

Compare Kulaśekhara's *Mukundamālā*:

jihve kīrtaya keśavaṁ muraripuṁ ceto bhaja śrīdharaṁ
pāṇidvandva samarcayācyutakathāḥ śrotradvaya tvaṁ śruṇu|
kṛṣṇaṁ lokaya locanadvaya harer gacchāṅghriyugmālayaṁ
jighra ghrāṇa mukundapādatulasīm mūrdhan namādhokṣajam||

"O tongue, sing the glory of Keśava! O mind, worship the Enemy of the demon Murā! O the two hands, serve the Lord of Śrī! O the two ears, hear the story of Acyuta! O the two eyes, behold Kṛṣṇa! O the two feet, go to the temple of Hari! O nose, smell the tulasī that is at the feet of Mukunda! O head, bow to the Lord Viṣṇu!

For *karau ca* there is an alternative reading: *karaś ca.*

8

यथा बुद्धिः शुक्तौ रजतमिति काचाश्मनि मणि-
जंले पैष्टे क्षीरं भवति मृगतृष्णासु सलिलम् ।
तथा देव भ्रान्त्या भजति भवदन्यं जडजनो
महादेवेशं त्वां मनसि च न मत्वा पशुपते ॥

yathā buddiḥ śuktau rajatam iti kācāśmani maṇir
jale paiṣṭe kṣiraṁ bhavati mṛgatṛṣṇāsu salilam|
tathā deva bhrāntyā bhajati bhavadanyaṁ jaḍajano
mahādeveśaṁ tvāṁ manasi ca na matvā paśupate||

O Great God! O Lord of souls! Just as one perceives nacre as silver, glass-bead as gem, water mixed with flour as milk, and mirage as water, so also the fool worships what is other than Thee under the delusion that it is deity, not contemplating Thee, the Lord, with the mind.

The ignorant worship the finite, leaving the Infinite, because of delusion. One values silver and mistakes nacre for silver because it resembles it. In all cases of delusion this is so. What one longs for is the Infinite. But one wrongly imagines that the finite objects of pleasure will afford one infinite happiness. Even the finite seems temporarily to please because it bears a reflection of the Infinite. He alone is wise who is not beguiled by the false appearances, and is constant in his devotion to the infinite Reality which is God.

9

गभीरे कासारे विशति विजने घोरविपने
विशाले शैले च भ्रमति कुसुमार्थं जडमतिः ।
समर्प्यैकं चेतः सरसिजमुमानाथ भवते
सुखेनावस्थातुं जन इह न जानाति किमहो ॥

gabhīre kāsāre viśati vijane ghoravipine
viśāle śaile ca bhramati kusumārthaṁ jaḍamatiḥ|
samarpyaikaṁ cetaḥsarasijam umānātha bhavate
sukhenāvasthātuṁ jana iha na jānāti kim aho||

O Lord of Umā! One gets into a deep tank, or enters into a fearful uninhabited forest, or roams on a high mountain in order to gather flowers — what a fool! Lo, he does not know how to live in happiness here, offering unto Thee the single heart-lotus!

Flower-offering to God as an act of worship has but a symbolic significance. God does not need to be decked with flowers. He is the supreme Beauty and does not require to be embellished. When the devotee offers a flower, it only means that he is offering his heart to God. Every ritual connected with worship has an inner meaning. What very often happens is that the inner meaning is forgotten and only the outer form is observed. In the present instance, flowers are offered to God with the erroneous belief that flowers please God. One may go through enormous hazards and hardships in order to pluck fiowers. But it is evident that all this endeavour is vain. What God wants is not a profusion of physical flowers but the single heart-lotus of the devotee.

10

नरत्वं देवत्वं नगवनमृगत्वं मशकता
पशुत्वं कीटत्वं भवतु विहगत्वादिजननम् ।
सदा त्वत्पादाब्जस्मरणपरमानन्दलहरी-
विहारासक्तं चेद्धृदयमिह किं तेन वपुषा ॥

naratvaṁ devatvaṁ nagavanamṛgatvaṁ maśakatā
paśutvaṁ kīṭatvaṁ bhavatu vihagatvādijananam|
sadā tvatpādābja-smaraṇa-paramānandalaharī
vihārāsaktaṁ ceddhṛdayam iha kim tena vapuṣā||

Let there be births as a human being, as a god, as a mountain, or forest-animal, as a mosquito, cow or worm, as a bird or as any other. If the heart, here, is ever given to sporting in the flood of supreme bliss consisting of the contemplation of Thy lotus-feet, what does it matter in which body one is born ?

If the heart has been given to God, then one need not worry about one's future. The next birth may be of any sort. One may be born in the sub-human, human, or super-human species. The kind of birth does not matter in the least, if in the present life one has surrendered oneself to God.

The Lord declares in the *Bhagavad-gītā*: "Those devotees who constantly worship Me, thinking of nothing else, and thus are ever united with Me in thought — for their welfare I bear the full responsibility" (ix, 22).

11

वटुर्वा गेही वा यतिरपि जटी वा तदितरो
नरो वा यः कश्चिद्भवतु भव किं तेन भवति ।
यदीयं हृत्पद्मं यदि भवदधीनं पशुपते
तदीयस्त्वं शंभो भवसि भवभारं च वहसि ॥

vaṭurvā gehī vā yatirapi jaṭī vā taditaro
naro vā yaḥ kaścidbhavatu bhava kiṁ tena bhavati/
yadīyaṁ hṛtpadmaṁ yadi bhavadadhīnaṁ paśupate
tadīyastvaṁ śaṁbho bhavasi bhavabhāraṁ ca vahasi//

O Lord! Let one be a student, a householder, a monk, an ascetic, or some other individual — of what use is it? O Lord of souls! O Śaṁbhu! when the heart-lotus of a person becomes thine, Thou dost become his; and Thou dost bear the burden of his life.

For the true devotee, not only does the kind of next birth not matter, but also the condition or state in which he is in the present birth. Devotion knows no distinctions of orders of life. The devotee may be a student, householder, ascetic or monk. These stages of life make no difference to him.

Nārada says in the *Bhakti-sūtra*, "Among the devotees there is not the distinction based on caste, learning, beauty, family, wealth, profession, and the rest" (*nāsti teṣu jāti-vidyā-rūpa-kula-dhana-kriyādi-bhedaḥ*).

12

गुहायां गेहे वा बहिरपि वने वाऽद्रिशिखरे
जले वा वह्नौ वा वसतु वसतेः किं वद फलम् ।
सदा यस्यैवान्तःकरणमपि शंभो तव पदे
स्थितं चेद्योगोऽसौ स च परमयोगी स च सुखी ॥

guhāyāṁ gehe vā bahirapi vane vā'driśikhare
jale vā vahnau vā vasatu vasateḥ kiṁ vada phalam|
sadā yasyaivāntaḥkaraṇam api śaṁbho tava pade
sthitaṁ cedyogo'sau sa ca paramayogī sa ca sukhī||

Let one live in a cave, in a house, in the open, in a forest, on the top of a mountain, in water, or in fire. Tell me, of what use is such living? O Śaṁbhu! If a person's mind remains always at Thy feet, that, verily, is *yoga*; he, indeed is the supreme *yogin*, yea, the one that is most happy!

The conditions under which one lives and the austerities one performs have no intrinsic value. What really matters is the mind's devotion to God. *Yoga* means yoking the mind; the true *yoga* is the yoking of the mind to God. When one thus becomes God-centred, one gains the supreme delight.

13

असारे संसारे निजभजनदूरे जडधिया
भ्रमन्तं मामन्धं परमकृपया पातुमुचितम् ।
मदन्यः को दीनस्तव कृपणरक्षातिनिपुण-
स्त्वदन्यः को वा मे त्रिजगति शरण्यः पशुपते ॥

asāre saṁsāre nijabhajanadūre jaḍadhiyā
bhramantaṁ māmandhaṁ paramakṛpayā pātumucitam|
madanyaḥ ko dīnastava kṛpaṇarakṣātinipuṇas
tvadanyaḥ ko vā me trijagati śaraṇyaḥ paśupate||

O Lord of souls! It is but proper that Thou shouldst protect me through Thy great compassion — me who am blind, and who revolve foolishly in the essenceless *saṁsāra* that is far away from one's real goal. To Thee, who can be poorer in spirit than I? And, to me, who can be a better expert than Thou, in protecting the poor and in offering refuge in all the three worlds?

The relation between the soul and God is an inseparable relation. The soul stands in need of protection; God is the supreme protector. When the soul does not realize this truth, it relies on false props in this world. Blinded by ignorance, it revolves in *saṁsāra*; and misery becomes its lot. When, however, devotion enters its heart, and it turns towards God, it receives sure succour and gets saved. The devotee is he who is convinced that God is his only help. For him, there is no saviour other than God in all the three worlds.

jaḍa-dhiyā may also be read as *ajaḍa dhiyā*. Then, the meaning would be: O the non-inert Spirit (*ajaḍa*), Thou shouldst protect me by granting wisdom (*dhī*).

14

प्रभुस्त्वं दीनानां खलु परमबन्धुः पशुपते
प्रमुख्योऽहं तेषामपि किमुत बन्धुत्वमनयोः ।
त्वयैव क्षन्तव्याः शिव मदपराधाश्च सकलाः
प्रयत्नात्कर्तव्यं मदवनमियं बन्धुसरणिः

prabhustvaṁ dīnānāṁ khalu paramabandhuḥ paśupate
pramukhyo'haṁ teṣām api kimuta bandhutvam anayoḥ/
tvayaiva kṣantavyāḥ śiva madaparādhāśca sakalāḥ
prayatnāt kartavyaṁ madavanam iyaṁ bandhusaraṇiḥ//

O Lord of souls! Art not Thou, who art the Lord, the greatest friend of the poor. And, of them, I am the foremost. Is not this, then, the relationship between us? O Siva! All my transgressions should be forgiven by Thee alone. Even through effort, protection should be given to me. This, indeed, is the way pursued by relations.

Here the devotee defines his relationship to God. He feels that by himself he is nothing; of the poor, he is the poorest. God is the Lord of all lords; above Him there is none. It is the soul's right to claim protection. And, it is God's duty to grant it. No offense that the soul has committed can free God from His obligation; for, it is His duty again to forgive the soul of all its sins.

15

उपेक्षा नो चेत्किं न हरसि भवद्ध्यानविमुखां
दुराशाभूयिष्ठां विधिलिपिमशक्तो यदि भवान् ।
शिरस्तद्वैधात्रं ननखलु सुवृत्तं पशुपते
कथं वा निर्यत्नं करनखमुखेनैव लुलितम् ॥

upekṣā no cet kiṁ na harasi bhavad-dhyāna-vimukhāṁ
durāśā-bhūyiṣṭhāṁ vidhilipim aśakto yadi bhavān|
śiras-tad-vaidhātraṁ nanakhalu suvṛttaṁ paśupate
kathaṁ vā niryatnaṁ karanakha-mukhenaiva lulitam||

O Lord of souls! If Thou art not indifferent (towards my lot), why is it that Thou dost not destroy the decree of Brahmā (in regard to me) that makes me turn away from meditating on Thee, and that fills me with evil desires? If Thou art powerless, how then was that head of Brahmā, which cannot be plucked with a thumb-nail and which is hard, plucked effortlessly by Thee with the merest tip of Thy thumb-nail?

God cannot throw the blame on fate and keep quiet. For, is He so powerless that He cannot set it right ? What can really stand against the might of God ? What can fate do as against the grace of God ?

In Hindu mythology, the deity that decrees fate is Brahmā, the creator. According to legend, Brahmā had originally five heads. But Śiva plucked off one of them. There are different versions of this legend. The *Varāha-purāṇa* says that Brahmā created Rudra and asked him to protect the world. While doing so, Brahmā addressed Rudra as *kapāli*, a term of insult. Rudra got angry and plucked off Brahmā's fifth head with his thumb-nail. The severed head stuck to Rudra's hand. The *Kūrma-purāṇa* has the following version: Once Brahmā was asked by the sages about the basic source of the universe. In reply, he proudly declared that he himself was the source. Śiva appeared on the scene and disputed Brahmā's claim. But Brahmā would not relent. A huge column of light flashed forth, and in it there was Śiva. Śiva ordered Bhairava to cut off one of the heads of Brahmā. When this was done, Brahmā's pride was quelled.

Śiva who is superior to Brahmā can certainly alter the fate of the devotee. What the devotee asks for is not escape from the consequences of his past deeds. He is quite prepared to take the punishments. What he asks God to remove is the bad *vāsanā* (tendency) that fills the heart with impure desires and turns it away from God.

16

विरिञ्चिर्दीर्घायुर्भवतु भवता तत्परशिर-
श्चतुष्कं संरक्ष्यं स खलु भुवि दैन्यं लिखितवान् ।
विचारः को वा मां विशदकृपया पाति शिव ते
कटाक्षव्यापारः स्वयमपि च दीनावनपरः ॥

viriñcir dīrghāyur bhavatu bhavatā tatparaśiraś-
catuṣkaṁ saṁrakṣyaṁ sa khalu bhuvi dainyaṁ likhitavān|
vicāraḥ ko vā māṁ viśadakṛpayā pāti śiva te
kaṭākṣavyāpāraḥ svayam api ca dīnāvanaparaḥ||

O Śiva, the pure one ! Let Brahmā live long ! Let the remaining four heads of his be protected by Thee! For, indeed, he has decreed (for me) poverty in this world. But what anxiety can there be for me, when the operation of Thy kindly glance which is always turned towards the poor will, out of its own accord, protect me.

If Brahmā has decreed poverty for any one, then that one should feel thankful to the creator. For, it is easy for one that is poor to turn to God for succour. And, God is the protector and friend of the poor (*dīna-rakṣakaḥ, dīna-bandhuḥ*).

May Brahmā live long, says the devotee; may Śiva spare him his other four heads!

17

फलाद्वा पुण्यानां मयि करुणया वा त्वयि विभो
प्रसन्नेऽपि स्वामिन् भवदमलपादाब्जयुगलम् ।
कथं पश्येयं मां स्थगयति नमःसंभ्रमजुषां
निलिम्पानां श्रेणिर्निजकनकमाणिक्यमुकुटैः ॥

phalād vā puṇyānāṁ mayi karuṇayā vā tvayi vibho
prasanne'pi svāmin bhavadamalapādābjayugalam|
kathaṁ paśyeyaṁ māṁ sthagayati namaḥsaṁbhramajuṣāṁ
nilimpānāṁ śreṇir nijakanakamāṇikyamukuṭaiḥ||

O, the all-pervading Master! Although either on account of the fruit of meritorious deeds, or through compassion for me, Thou art graciously present, how am I to behold Thy blemishless lotus-feet? The whole gathering of gods, who press forward in their eagerness to make obeisance to Thee, prevent me (from beholding Thy feet) by the splendour of their golden tiaras set with gems.

The devotee may come into the presence of God either on account of past merit or on account of divine grace. But there is no guarantee that he will behold the holy feet of God. For, a crowd of gods is there surrounding the feet and offering obeisance to them. Added to the density of the gods is the dazzling effect of their gem-set crowns.

This is the poetic way of saying that Śiva is the supreme Deity, the God of gods (*deva-deva*), the great God (*mahādeva*).

18

त्वमेको लोकानां परमफलदो दिव्यपदवीं
वहन्तस्त्वन्मूलां पुनरपि भजन्ते हरिमुखाः ।
कियद्वा दाक्षिण्यं तव शिव मदाशा च कियती
कदा वा मद्रक्षां वहसि करुणापूरितदृशा ॥

tvam eko lokānāṁ paramaphalado divyapadavīṁ
vahantas tvanmūlāṁ punarapi bhajante harimukhāḥ|
kiyad vā dākṣiṇyaṁ tava śiva madāśā ca kiyatī
kadā vā madrakṣāṁ vahasi karuṇā-pūrita-dṛśā||

O Śiva! Thou art the sole supreme benefactor of all beings. Viṣṇu and other gods, who occupy their present divine status through Thee, beseech Thee again (either for maintaining their status or for improving it). How great is Thy Grace! And, how great is my desire! When wilt Thou perform the function of protecting me through Thy look laden with compassion ?

The various gods owe their greatness to Śiva. They pray to Him for preserving their gains and for making further progress. Śiva is the source of all blessings, the benefactor of all beings. The devotee appeals to Śiva for the bestowal of His grace upon him.

19

दुराशाभूयिष्ठे दुरधिपगृहद्वारघटके
दुरन्ते संसारे दुरितनिलये दुःखजनके ।

मदायासं किं न व्यपनयसि कस्योपकृतये
वदेयं प्रीतिश्चेत्तव शिव कृतार्थाः खलु वयम् ॥

durāśā-bhūyiṣṭhe duradhipa-gṛhadvāra-ghaṭake
durante saṁsāre duritanilaye duḥkhajanake|
madāyāsaṁ kiṁ na vyapanayasi kasyopakṛtaye
vadeyaṁ prītiścet tava śiva kṛtārthāḥ khalu vayam||

Is it for benefiting Brahmā that Thou wilt not remove my suffering in *saṁsāra* which brims with evil desires, which leads to the doorsteps of evil rulers, which is endless, which is the home of sin, and which generates misery? Tell me, O Śiva! If this be Thy pleasure, we shall, indeed, be blessed!

It is by God's grace that one's bad tendencies and evil nature could be changed. There is nothing that God cannot transmute. The decrees of Fate have no validity before the grace of God.

It is to be noted that among the bad effects of evil fate is mentioned seeking the patronage of wicked rulers.

20

सदा मोहाटव्यां चरति युवतीनां कुचगिरौ
नटत्याशाशाखास्वटति झटिति स्वैरमभितः ।
कपालिन् भिक्षो मे हृदयकपिमत्यन्तचपलं
दृढं भक्त्या बद्ध्वा शिव भवदधीनं कुरु विभो ॥

sadā mohāṭavyāṁ carati yuvatīnāṁ kucagirau
naṭaty āśāśākhāsv aṭati jhaṭiti svairam-abhitaḥ|
kapālin bhikṣo me hṛdaya-kapim atyanta-capalaṁ
dṛḍhaṁ bhaktyā baddhvā śiva bhavad-adhīnaṁ kuru vibho||

O Śiva, bearing the skull (as alms-bowl)! O the One that is all-pervading! O Mendicant! It ever roams the forest of delusion, dances on the breast-hills of maidens, leaps quickly in all directions, and as it likes, from branch to branch of desires—extremely inconstant is this monkey-mind of mine! (Accepting it as my alms-offering) bind it firmly with the cord of devotion, and bring it under Thy control!

Here, the mind is compared to a monkey. Whether the Darwinian theory of man's descent from the ape is true or not, there is doubtless similarity between the behaviour of the human mind and the roving activity of the monkey. Driven by desires, prompted by passions, the mind moves from object to object; it whirls in a wayward manner, finding no rest or peace.

The mind can be controlled through devotion to God. Among the many roles that Śiva plays is the one in which He goes about as a mendicant (*bhikṣu*) with a skull for almsbowl, begging for alms. In this verse, the Lord is implored to accept the mind-monkey as an offering. If only He would bind this monkey with the cord of devotion and keep it under control, He would receive plenty of alms.

21

धृतिस्तम्भाधारां दृढगुणनिबद्धां सगमनां
विचित्रां पद्माढ्यां प्रतिदिवससन्मार्गघटिताम् ।
स्मरारे मच्चेतःस्फुटपटकुटीं प्राप्य विशदां
जय स्वामिन् शक्त्या सह शिवगणैः सेवित विभो ॥

dhṛtistambhādhārāṁ dṛḍhaguṇanibaddhāṁ sagamanāṁ
vicitrāṁ padmāḍhyāṁ pratidivasa-sanmārga-ghaṭitām|
smarāre maccetaḥsphuṭapaṭakuṭīṁ prāpya viśadāṁ
jaya svāmin śaktyā saha śivagaṇaiḥ sevita vibho||

O Destroyer of Manmatha! O Master! O Śiva, that art worshipped by the divine attendants! O the all-pervading One! Enter along with Thy consort the shining tent of my mind, that has the will as the supporting central pole, and is fastened with the ropes of constant virtues, that could be moved anywhere, is multi-coloured, and is embellished with the figures of lotuses and is moved daily on highways; and mayest Thou be victorious!

The mind is compared, here, to a strong, clean, and well-furnished tent; and the Lord is invited to use it in his campaign against evil. The entry of the Lord along with His Consort into the tent will ensure victory over evil. Let not the mind-tent be allowed to fall into the hands of the enemy!

22

प्रलोभाद्यैरर्थाहरणपरतन्त्रो धनिगृहे
प्रवेशोद्युक्तः सन् भ्रमति बहुधा तस्करपते ।
इमं चेतश्चोरं कथमिह सहे शंकरविभो
तवाधीनं कृत्वा मयि निरपराधे कुरु कृपाम् ॥

pralobhādyair arthāharaṇa-paratantro dhanigṛhe
praveśodyuktaḥ san bhramati bahudhā taskarapate|
imaṁ cetaścoraṁ katham iha sahe śaṅkaravibho
tavādhīnaṁ kṛtvā mayi niraparādhe kuru kṛpām||

O Śaṅkara ! O Arch-Thief ! O all-pervading One ! This thief of a mind roams about widely, having fallen a victim to the business of amassing wealth through greed, etc., and making efforts to break into the houses of the rich. How can I suffer him ? Having brought him under Thy control, please bestow grace on me who am innocent !

The mind is like a thief, intent always on practising deceit and fraud. Everyone of the mental modes may be compared to a thief; attachments, aversions, avarice, anger, etc., are thieves in the sense that they rob one of the discriminating wisdom.

Who can put a curb on the mind except the Lord? He is the lord of thieves, (1) as He is the lord of the universe, and (2) as He steals the hearts of the devotees. The Veda offers obeisance to Rudra-Śiva as the chief of thieves (*taskarāṇāṁ pataye namaḥ*).

23

करोमि त्वत्पूजां सपदि सुखदो मे भव विभो
विधित्वं विष्णुत्वं दिशसि खलु तस्याः फलमिति ।
पुनश्च त्वां द्रष्टुं दिवि भुवि वहन् पक्षिमृगता-
मदृष्ट्वा तत्खेदं कथमिह सहे शंकरविभो ॥

karomi tvatpūjāṁ sapadi sukhado me bhava vibho
vidhitvaṁ viṣṇutvaṁ diśasi khalu tasyāḥ phalam iti|
punaśca tvāṁ draṣṭuṁ divi bhuvi vahan pakṣimṛgatām
adṛṣṭvā tatkhedaṁ katham iha sahe śaṅkaravibho||

O Śaṅkara, the all-pervading One! I perform Thy worship; and please grant me immediately the (supreme) happiness! Shouldst Thou grant me the status of Brahmā or Viṣṇu as the fruit of my worship, I would only have the agony of taking the form of bird or animal for the sake of seeing Thee in heaven or on earth, again, and of not seeing Thee! How can I bear this (agony), O all-pervading Lord!

The true devotee longs for release (*mokṣa*) from bondage as the fruit of his devotion. Nothing less will satisfy him — not even the status of the high gods such as Viṣṇu and Brahmā.

The story alluded to here relates to the failure of these two gods to discover the head and feet of Śiva. Brahmā and Viṣṇu once had an argument about their relative superiority. Śiva appeared before them in the form of a pillar of light — luminous

Liṅga—without visible top or bottom. Brahmā and Viṣṇu entered into an agreement according to which they were to seek to find the limits of the Liṅga, and he who succeeded in this effort would be regarded as the superior god. Viṣṇu took the form of a boar and burrowed into the earth in order to get to the foot of the Liṅga. Brahmā assumed the form of a swan and flew up to reach its crown. Neither of them succeeded. Their pride humbled, they prayed to the Lord of lords, recognizing Him as the supreme Deity.

Tradition believes that the Aruṇācala hill at Tiruvaṇṇāmalai represents the pillar of light in which form Śiva appeared before Brahmā and Viṣṇu.

In several verses of the *Śivānandalaharī*, Śaṅkara alludes to the story of the failure of Brahmā and Viṣṇu to gauge the greatness of Śiva.

24

कदा वा कैलासे कनकमणिसौधे सह गणै-
र्वसन् शंभोरग्रे स्फुटघटितमूर्धाञ्जलिपुटः ।
विभो साम्ब स्वामिन् परमशिव पाहीति निगद-
न्विधातॄणां कल्पान् क्षणमिव विनेष्यामि सुखतः ॥

kadā vā kailāse kanakamaṇisaudhe saha gaṇair
vasan śaṁbhor agre sphuṭaghaṭita-mūrdhāñjalipuṭaḥ|
vibho sāmba svāmin paramaśiva pāhīti nigadan
vidhātṝṇāṁ kalpān kṣaṇam iva vineṣyāmi sukhataḥ||

When shall I live in Kailāśa, in the Hall of gold and emeralds, in the company of the divine attendants, in the presence of Śaṁbhu, and with folded hands gleaming on my head, addressing thus "O the all-pervading One! O, the One with the Devī! O Master! O the supreme Śiva! Protect me!" and spend in happiness aeons of Brahmās as if they were seconds ?

Here is a grand vision of Kailāśa, the Abode of Śiva. It is the realm of eternity where time counts not. When one is engaged in adoring Śiva, one is not weighed down by the oppressive sense of time.

Variant readings:
For the second line,
vasan śaṁbho mūrdhasphuṭa-ghaṭitabaddhāñjali-puṭaḥ.
For *kṣaṇamiva vineṣyāmi*, *nimiṣamiva neṣyāmi.*

25

स्तवैर्ब्रह्मादीनां जयजयवचोभिर्नियमिनां
गणानां केलीभिर्मदकलमहोक्षस्य ककुदि ।
स्थितं नीलग्रीवं त्रिनयनमुमाश्लिष्टवपुषं
कदा त्वां पश्येयं करधृतमृगं खण्डपरशुम् ।।

stavair brahmādīnāṁ jayajayavacobhir niyamināṁ
gaṇānāṁ kelībhir madakala-mahokṣasya kakudi|
sthitaṁ nīlagrīvaṁ trinayanam umāśliṣṭavapuṣaṁ
kadā tvāṁ paśyeyaṁ karadhṛtamṛgaṁ khaṇḍaparaśum||

When shall I behold Thee, that hast a blue throat, three eyes and a body embraced by Umā, that holdest in Thy hands a deer and a cutting axe, that art seated on the hump of the big bull that is lusty and handsome, as Brahmā and other gods sing Thy praise, as the ascetics cry out "Hail! Hail!", and as the divine attendants dance around?

The devotee prays for the vision of Kailāśa.

Among the characteristics mentioned are: the blue throat, three eyes, and the half male-half female form — all indicative of infinite grace. There can be no sorrow in Kailāśa; all is mirth and joy. All grades of beings lose their individualities and sense of separateness in the presence of Śiva. While singing the praise of Śiva or dancing in ecstasy, they forget themselves. Kailāśa is the glorious experience of divine grace.

26

कदा वा त्वां दृष्ट्वा गिरिश तव भव्याङ्घ्रियुगल
गृहीत्वा हस्ताभ्यां शिरसि नयने वक्षसि वहन् ।
समाश्लिष्याघ्राय स्फुटजलजगन्धान् परिमला-
नलभ्यां ब्रह्माद्यैर्मुदमनुभविष्यामि हृदये ॥

kadā vā tvāṁ dṛṣṭvā giriśa tava bhavyāṅghriyugalaṁ
gṛhītvā hastābhyāṁ śirasi nayane vakṣasi vahan|
samāśliṣyāghrāya sphuṭajalajagandhān parimalān
alabhyāṁ brahmādyair mudam-anubhaviṣyāmi hṛdaye||

O Mountain-Dweller! Beholding Thee, and holding with my hands Thy gracious Feet, pressing them against my head, eyes, and chest, embracing them, and smelling the sweet scents of the full-blown lotuses, when am I to enjoy the happiness that does not come even to Brahmā and others?

It is Śiva that should fill one's body, senses, and mind. The pleasure that one derives from sense-objects is nothing compared with the joy that comes from Śiva. The devotee longs for the constant presence of, contact with, and dissolution in Śiva.

27

करस्थे हेमाद्रौ गिरिश निकटस्थे धनपतौ
गृहस्थे स्वर्भूजामरसुरभिचिन्तामणिगणे ।
शिरस्थे शीतांशौ चरणयुगलस्थेऽखिलशुभे
कमर्थं दास्येऽहं भवतु भवदर्थं मम मनः ॥

karasthe hemādrau giriśa nikaṭasthe dhanapatau
gṛhasthe svarbhūjāmarasurabhicintāmaṇigaṇe|
śirasthe śītāṁśau caraṇayugalasthe 'khilaśubhe
kamarthaṁ dāsye'haṁ bhavatu bhavadarthaṁ mama manaḥ||

O Mountain-Dweller! When the golden mountain (Meru) is in Thy hands (as bow), when the lord of wealth (Kubera) stays near Thee (as Thy servant), when in Thy household are the heavenly trees, the divine cow, and wish-granting gems, when the cool moon is on Thy head, and when everything that is auspicious is at Thy Feet, what tribute can I give Thee? May my mind be dedicated to Thee!

There is nothing of value that we can give to Śiva; for He is the source of all value. What has He not that we could offer Him? All auspiciousness flows from His feet. He does not require our wealth or material offerings. These are themselves the gifts of His grace. What we should offer to Him is our mind. Let our wills be dedicated to Him. Let our passions run to Him. Let our thoughts dwell on Him.

28

सारूप्यं तव पूजने शिव महादेवेति संकीर्तने
सामीप्यं शिवभक्तिधुर्यजनतासाङ्गत्यसंभाषणे ।
सालोक्यं च चराचरात्मकतनुध्याने भवानीपते
सायुज्यं मम सिद्धमत्र भवति स्वामिन्कृतार्थोऽस्म्यहम् ॥

sārūpyaṁ tava pūjane śiva mahādeveti saṅkīrtane
sāmīpyaṁ śivabhaktidhuryajanatā-sāṅgatyasaṁbhāṣaṇe|
sālokyaṁ ca carācarātmakatanudhyāne bhavānīpate
sāyujyaṁ mama siddham atra bhavati svāmin kṛtārtho' smyaham||

O Consort of Pārvatī! Sameness of form (*sārūpya*) through worshipping Thee, nearness (*sāmīpya*) through singing Thy names 'Śiva, Mahādeva', sameness of residence (*sālokya*) through conversation with, and the company of, people who are experts in Śiva-devotion, and union (*sāyujya*) through meditation on Thy Form which comprises all beings, moving and non-moving, become accomplished by me, even here. O Master ! I have, indeed, achieved my end!

Although there are no grades in *mukti* (final release), there are different levels in the experience of *Īśvara* or *Saguṇa-Brahman.* Four levels are usually distinguished: (1) *sālokya* (sameness of residence with God), (2) *sāmīpya* (nearness to God), (3) *sārūpya* (sameness of form), and (4) *sāyujya* (union). In the Śaiva schools four means to Godhead are recognized, *caryā*, *kriyā*, *yoga* and *jñāna*. *Caryā* is the path of works consisting in cleaning the temples, serving God's devotees, etc. *Kriyā* is the path of ritual worship. *Yoga* is the path of contemplation and meditation. *Jñāna* is the path of knowledge and realization of God. The four Tamil saints, Appar, Jñāna-sambandhar, Sundarar, and Māṇikkavācakar are said to be the exemplars of these paths, respectively.

In the present verse, the four levels of God-experience are mentioned, and the modes of gaining them are indicated.

29

त्वत्पादाम्बुजमर्चयामि परमं त्वां चिन्तयाम्यन्वहं
त्वामीशं शरणं व्रजामि वचसा त्वामेव याचे विभो ।
वीक्षां मे दिश चाक्षुषीं सकरुणां दिव्यैश्चिरं प्रार्थितां
शंभो लोकगुरो मदीयमनसः सौख्योपदेशं कुरु ॥

tvatpādāmbujam arcayāmi paramaṁ tvāṁ cintayāmy anvahaṁ
tvāmīśaṁ śaraṇaṁ vrajāmi vacasā tvām eva yāce vibho|
vīkṣāṁ me diśa cākṣuṣīṁ sakaruṇāṁ divyaiś ciraṁ prārthitāṁ
śaṁbho lokaguro madīyamanasaḥ saukhyopadeśaṁ kuru||

O all-pervading One! I worship Thy lotus-feet; I meditate daily on Thee that art supreme; I seek refuge in Thee that art the Lord; through words I beg of Thee alone; cast on me the look of Thy eyes that are full of grace, the look for which the gods have been praying for long. O Śaṁbhu! O world-Teacher! Give to my mind the instruction about happiness!

Śiva, the world-teacher, is besought here for instruction in the mode of gaining release. In order to receive the instruction, one has to surrender oneself to Him. It is complete self-surrender that will elicit grace from God. And, it is through the divine grace that the liberating wisdom can be gained.

Compare the *Bhagavad-gītā*, ii, 7, where Arjuna makes the supplication to Śrī Kṛṣṇa:

yacchreyaḥ syānniścitaṁ brūhi tan me
śiṣyaste'haṁ śādhi māṁ tvāṁ prapannam|

(Tell me that which is decidedly good; I am thy disciple. Do instruct me, who have sought refuge in Thee.)

Also, see *Bhagavad-gītā*, xi, 43:

pitāsi lokasya carācarasya
tvam asya pūjyaśca gururgarīyān|
na tvatsamo'styabhyadhikaḥ kuto'nyo
lokatraye'pyapratimaprabhāva||

(Of this world consisting of moving and non-moving creatures, Thou art Father, the Adorable, and the great Teacher; in all the three worlds, there is no one who is equal to Thee; how can there be anyone superior, O Possessor of incomparable splendour!)

30

वस्त्रोद्‌धूतविधौ सहस्रकरता पुष्पार्चने विष्णुता
गन्धे गन्धवहात्मतान्नपचने बर्हिर्मखाध्यक्षता ।
पात्रे काञ्चनगर्भतास्ति मयि चेद्‌बालेन्दुचूडामणे
शुश्रूषां करवाणि ते पशुपते स्वामिंस्त्रिलोकीगुरो ।।

vastroddhūtavidhau sahasrakaratā puṣpārcane viṣṇutā
gandhe gandhavahātmatānnapacane barhirmakhādhyakṣatā|
pātre kāñcanagarbhatāsti mayi ced bālenducūḍāmaṇe
śuśrūṣāṁ karavāṇi te paśupate svāmiṁstrilokīguro||

O, the One who wearest the young moon as crest-jewel! O Lord of souls! O Master! O Teacher of the three worlds! If there be in me the status of the sun with a thousand hands (rays) in the matter of dressing Thee in clothes, the status of Viṣṇu in the matter of worshipping Thee with flowers, the status of Vāyu in the matter of applying sandal-paste (to Thy body), the status of Indra, the chief of Agni, in the matter of cooking food, and the status of Hiraṇyagarbha in the matter of making vessels, then may I render service to Thee!

In the previous verse, Śiva was addressed as the world-teacher (*loka-guru*). In the present verse, he is called the teacher of the three worlds (*trilokī-guru*).

In order to gain Śiva's grace, one has to worship Him. But how is it possible for the limited individual to worship Him? God is infinite; the individual is finite. How can the finite individual perform even formal worship consisting of offering to God, cloth, flowers, sandal-paste, cooked food, etc.? In order to be able to do this, the finite individual should rise to the status of the gods such as Sūrya, Viṣṇu, Vāyu, and Indra.

31

नालं वा परमोपकारकमिदं त्वेकं पशूनां पते
पश्यन्कुक्षिगतांश्चराचरगणान्बाह्यस्थितान्रक्षितुम् ।
सर्वामर्त्यपलायनौषधमतिज्वालाकरं भीकरं
निक्षिप्तं गरलं गले न गिलितं नोद्गीर्णमेव त्वया ॥

nālaṁ vā paramopakārakam idaṁ tvekaṁ paśūnāṁ pate
paśyan kukṣigatāṁścarācaragaṇān bāhyasthitān rakṣitum|

sarvāmartyapalāyanauṣadham atijvālākaraṁ bhīkaraṁ
nikṣiptaṁ garalaṁ gale na gilitaṁ nodgīrṇam eva tvayā||

O Lord of souls, Is not this single supreme deed of help enough (to proclaim Thy mercy)? With a view to protect the beings, moving and non-moving residing inside Thy stomach, as well as outside, Thou didst place in Thy throat the flaming and fearful poison that was making all the gods run for life; it was neither taken in nor thrown out !

In this verse and the next, Śiva is praised as the sole benefactor of the world. So often is Śiva regarded as the world-destroyer that His role as protector is seldom remembered.

In the Purāṇas the story is told, of how Śiva saved all beings by swallowing the *Hālāhala* poison. The gods and the demons churned the milk-ocean with a view to gain therefrom the ambrosia that would make them immortal. But the first object to arise out of the churning was the world-destroying poison, *Hālāhala*. The gods and the demons alike took to their heels, dreading death. Out of great compassion Śiva came to their rescue, took the poison in His hand and placed it in His mouth, in order to save them; if the poison went into His stomach, the creatures residing there would be destroyed; so, He retained the poison in His throat. As a consequence, His white throat became blue or dark. Hence, the epithets: *Nīlakaṇṭha*, *Kāḷakaṇṭha*, *Nīlagrīva*. The blue throat of the Lord reveals His beauty and auspicious nature: He is *Śrīkaṇṭha*.

Here are two verses from Sundaramūrti's *Tēvāram*:

"When the celestials used the serpent that bites and the mountain to churn the ocean, there emerged poison. Fearing that it might destroy the worlds, You Yourself took that poison as nectar—nor did You spit it out. You are the beautiful one presiding over Tirupputtūr". (7, 8, 10).

When the beautiful mountain and serpent were used as churning rod and rope respectively to churn the ocean, deadly poison emerged. As the assembled persons took to their heels in fear,

You thought of saving the celestials and, the mad one that You are, You took the poison and kept it in Your throat. Oh Lord of Tiruppuṅkūr, seeing this virtuous conduct of Yours, I have come to Your feet (as my refuge)." (7, 55, 5.).

32

ज्वालोग्रः सकलामरातिभयदः क्ष्वेलः कथं वा त्वया
दृष्टः किं च करे धृतः करतले किं पक्वजम्बूफलम् ।
जिह्वायां निहितश्च सिद्धघुटिका वा कण्ठदेशे भृतः
किं ते नीलमणिर्विभूषणमयं शंभो महात्मन्वद ॥

jvālograḥ sakalāmarātibhayadaḥ kṣvelaḥ kathaṁ vā tvayā
dṛṣṭaḥ kiṁ ca kare dhṛtaḥ karatale kiṁ pakvajambūphalam|
jihvāyāṁ nihitaśca siddhaghuṭikā vā kaṇṭhadeśe bhṛtaḥ
kiṁ te nīlamaṇir vibhūṣaṇamayaṁ śaṁbho mahātman vada||

O Śaṁbhu! How was the poison that was flaming and was causing fear to all the gods, looked upon by Thee? And, how was it borne by Thee in the hand? Was it a ripe rose-apple in the palm of Thy hand? Or, was it a medicine used by *Siddhas*? It was retained in the throat: Was it a blue gem ornament? Tell me, O Great One!

Judged by our standards, the drinking of the poison by Śiva is not an easily explainable act. Unless by mistake, or unless one wished to die, one would not swallow poison. Did not Śiva realize that the *Hālāhala* was the deadliest of poisons? Did He not see that even the gods were fleeing from it? Did He imagine that it was an edible fruit, or a curative pill, or a brilliant gem? The wonder-act of the Lord is past our understanding. What great compassion, what profound solicitude for the safety and security of His creatures!

33

नालं वा सकृदेव देव भवतः सेवा नतिर्वा नुतिः
पूजा वा स्मरणं कथाश्रवणमप्यालोकनं मादृशाम् ।

स्वामिन्नस्थिरदेवतानुसरणायासेन किं लभ्यते
का वा मुक्तिरितः कुतो भवति चेत्किं प्रार्थनीयं तदा ॥

nālaṁ vā sakṛdeva deva bhavataḥ sevā natir vā nutiḥ
pūjā vā smaraṇaṁ kathāśravaṇam apy ālokanaṁ mādṛśām|
svāminnasthiradevatānusaraṇāyāsena kiṁ labhyate
kā vā muktir itaḥ kuto bhavati cet kiṁ prārthanīyaṁ tadā||

O Master ! O God ! Is it not enough for people like me to serve Thee even once through making obeisance, singing praise, worship, meditation, listening to Thy story, or having a sight of Thee? Other than thus, how is release possible ? This being so, what is to be gained by following, with effort, gods who are impermanent ? And why should they be prayed to ?

The devotee is convinced that nothing else is required for gaining release than the grace of Śiva. Even a single act of worship offered to Him in all sincerity is enough. Why go to the other gods and godlings ? What independent power do they possess ? Any effort to court them will only end in futility and frustration.

34

किं ब्रूमस्तव साहसं पशुपते कस्यास्ति शंभो भव-
द्धैर्यं चेदृशमात्मनः स्थितिरियं चान्यैः कथं लभ्यते ।
भ्रश्यद्देवगणं त्रसन्मुनिगणं नश्यत्प्रपञ्चं लयं
पश्यन्निर्भय एक एव विहरत्यानन्दसान्द्रो भवान् ॥

kiṁ brūmas tava sāhasaṁ paśupate kasyāsti śambho bhavad
dhairyaṁ cedṛśam ātmanaḥ sthitir iyaṁ cānyaiḥ kathaṁ labhyate|
bhraśyaddevagaṇaṁ trasanmunigaṇaṁ naśyatprapañcaṁ layaṁ
paśyan nirbhaya eka eva viharaty ānandasāndro bhavān||

O Lord of souls ! What shall we say about Thy exploits ? O Śaṁbhu ! Who can possess Thy courage in this manner? How can this status of Thine be obtained by others? Beholding the state of dissolution, when the gods fall (from their positions), the ascetics are seized with fright, and the world gets destroyed, Thou dost revel all alone, without fear, and filled with bliss.

The Śaiva texts give this as one of the arguments for establishing the supremacy of Śiva: at the time of dissolution when all beings are destroyed, He alone remains without any mutation. He is 'the still-point of a turning world'. The entire universe passes away. But that makes no difference to Him. It is only when there is another that there is fear for one. Since Śiva is the non-dual reality, He is fearless and of the nature of bliss. His happiness is not fugitive and contingent. He is happiness itself. His revelry is not object-conditioned; He is *ātmā-rāma*.

35

योगक्षेमधुरंधरस्य सकलश्रेयःप्रदोद्योगिनो
दृष्टादृष्टमतोपदेशकृतिनो बाह्यान्तरव्यापिनः ।
सर्वज्ञस्य दयाकरस्य भवतः किं वेदितव्यं मया
शंभो त्वं परमान्तरङ्ग इति मे चित्ते स्मराम्यन्वहम् ॥

yogakṣemadhuraṁdharasya sakalaśreyaḥ pradodyogino
dṛṣṭādṛṣṭamatopadeśakṛtino bāhyāntaravyāpinaḥ|
sarvajñasya dayākarasya bhavataḥ kiṁ veditavyaṁ mayā
śaṁbho tvaṁ paramāntaraṅga iti me citte smarāmy anvaham||

O Śaṁbhu! Thou bearest the responsibility for the welfare (of all beings); Thou art intent on giving all that is good; Thou dost teach the way to all desired ends, seen and unseen; Thou art all-pervading, inside and outside; Thou art omniscient and merciful: to Thee, what should I make known? Thou art my inmost self: thus do I always think in my mind.

Śiva is the source of all auspiciousness. He is the giver of all good, and the guarantor of the welfare of all. He saves the soul by imparting to it the knowledge of what is good, and by revealing the supreme truth. He is omnipresent, omniscient, and compassionate. Where is the need for the devotee to make known anything to Him? For, He knows all. The only task that the devotee should do is to remember the greatness of Śiva, and to realize that He is the inner ruler immortal.

36

भक्तो भक्तिगुणावृते मुदमृतापूर्णे प्रसन्ने मनः-
कुम्भे साम्ब तवाङ्घ्रिपल्लवयुगं संस्थाप्य संवित्फलम् ।
सत्त्वं मन्त्रमुदीरयन्निजशरीरागारशुद्धिं वह-
न्पुण्याहं प्रकटीकरोमि रुचिरं कल्याणमापादयन् ॥

bhakto bhaktiguṇāvṛte mudamṛtāpūrṇe prasanne manaḥ
kumbhe sāmba tavāṅghripallavayugaṁ saṁsthāpya saṁvitphalam|
sattvaṁ mantram udīrayan nijaśarīrāgāraśuddhiṁ vahan
puṇyāhaṁ prakaṭīkaromi ruciraṁ kalyāṇam āpādayan||

O Sāmba! Entwining with the cord of devotion, filling with the water of joy, in the shining pot of mind, I, who am a devotee, place the two tender leaves of Thy Feet; keep thereon the cocoanut of wisdom; utter the sacred formulas of goodness; purify the house of my body: thus do I perform the *puṇyāha* rite, occasioning the supreme blessedness.

The ritual called *puṇyāha* is performed for purifying a place. The purpose of this rite is the removal of inauspiciousness and impurity. A pitcher is wound with thread, and filled with water. Mango leaves are placed in its mouth, and on them a cocoanut is kept. The appropriate *mantras* are uttered, and ritual acts performed. Finally, the sanctified water from the pitcher is sprinkled all over the place, taking it out with the mango leaves. This is the outer *puṇyāha*. In the present verse, the inner *puṇyāha* is explained. By this process are the body, sense-organs and mind purified, and the final intuition which liberates the soul is gained. There is a symbolic side to every ritual. The Upaniṣads explain the symbolic significance of some of the Vedic rituals. At the commencement of the *Bṛhadāraṇyaka*, for instance, there is a symbolic description of the Horse-sacrifice (*Aśvamedha*).

37

आम्नायाम्बुधिमादरेण सुमनःसंघाः समुद्यन्मनो-
मन्थानं दृढभक्तिरज्जुसहितं कृत्वा मथित्वा ततः ।
सोमं कल्पतरुं सुपर्वसुरभिं चिन्तामणिं धीमतां
नित्यानन्दसुधां निरन्तररमासौभाग्यमातन्वते ॥

āmnāyāmbudhim ādareṇa sumanaḥsaṅghāḥ samudyanmano
manthānaṁ dṛḍhabhaktirajjusahitaṁ kṛtvā mathitvā tataḥ|
somaṁ kalpataruṁ suparvasurabhiṁ cintāmaṇiṁ dhīmatāṁ
nityānandasudhāṁ nirantararamāsaubhāgyam ātanvate||

Making the resolute intelligence the churning rod with the rope of firm devotion attached, those of good mind churn the ocean of Scripture with eagerness, and obtain therefrom the Moon, the wish-fulfilling tree, the cow of plenty, the wish-yielding gem, the ambrosia of eternal bliss, the perennial delightful Blessedness pertaining to the wise.

The story of the churning of the milk-ocean is allegorized here. Out of the milk-ocean arose auspicious objects, delightful things — each fulfilling some wish or desire of man. The inquiry into the purport of Scripture with a resolute intelligence and firm devotion yields, not a variety of ends, but the final goal which is *mokṣa*. *Soma*, *kalpavṛkṣa*, *kāmadhenu*, *cintāmaṇi*, *amṛta*, *Lakṣmī* — all of them, here, stand for one and the same objective which is release, the supreme beatitude.

38

प्राक्पुण्याचलमार्गदर्शितसुधामूर्तिः प्रसन्नः शिवः
सोमः सद्गणसेवितो मृगधरः पूर्णस्तमोमोचकः ।
चेतःपुष्करलक्षितो भवति चेदानन्दपाथोनिधिः
प्रागल्भ्येन विजृम्भते सुमनसां वृत्तिस्तदा जायते ॥

prākpuṇyācalamārgadarśitasudhāmūrtiḥ prasannaḥ śivaḥ
somaḥ sadgaṇasevito mṛgadharaḥ pūrṇastamomocakaḥ|
cetaḥpuṣkaralakṣito bhavati cedānanda-pāthonidhiḥ
prāgalbhyena vijṛmbhate sumanasāṁ vṛttis tadā jāyate||

(1) When the clear auspicious Moon bearing the figure of the deer rises with a white form seen through the opening in the eastern mountains, accompanied by the stars, releasing (the world) from dense darkness, and casting its reflection in the lucid lake, then the delightful ocean leaps magnificently, and a way of living becomes possible for people who are diligent.
(2) When the tranquil Śiva holding the deer in his hand appears with an immortal form on account of the mountain-like merit acquired earlier, accompanied by the gods, releasing (the world) from primal ignorance, and being felt in the mind, then Brahman-Bliss becomes clearly manifest, and a transformation takes place in the hearts of the good.

There is a pun on the words constituting this verse. The words apply to the moon as well as to Śiva. The two functions that the moon fulfils are removing darkness and giving delight. Śiva's grace liberates the soul from primal ignorance and grants it the plenary happiness. Śiva is the transcendent divine Moon. The term *Soma* also means 'the One who has Umā by His side', viz. Śiva.

39

धर्मो मे चतुरङ्घ्रिकः सुचरितः पापं विनाशं गतं
कामक्रोधमदादयो विगलिताः कालाः सुखाविष्कृताः ।
ज्ञानानन्दमहौषधिः सुफलिता कैवल्यनाथे सदा
मान्ये मानसपुण्डरीकनगरे राजावतंसे स्थिते ॥

dharmo me caturaṅghrikaḥ sucaritaḥ pāpaṁ vināśaṁ gataṁ
kāmakrodhamadādayo vigalitāḥ kālāḥ sukhāviṣkṛtāḥ|
jñānānandamahauṣadhiḥ suphalitā kaivalyanāthe sadā
mānye mānasapuṇḍarīkanagare rājāvataṁse sthite||

When the worshipful Lord of perfection who bears the Moon as crest-jewel (the great king) is crowned in the esteemed city of mind-lotus, the four-footed *dharma* becomes whole, sin gets destroyed, passions such as lust, anger, and pride are removed, the times begin to manifest happiness, the crops of wisdom and bliss become plentiful.

Many thinkers have dreamt of political Utopias. The ideal state is that in which there is perfect rectitude. Justice and harmony contentment and peace would prevail in such a state. Virtue, and not force, would be its foundation. The term *Rāma-rājya* signifies the ideal State.

Saints and sages have given us a vision of *Civitas Dei*, the City of God, the kingdom of Heaven. Śiva is the king of kings. When he makes the mind His capital-city and takes His residence there, all will be well with the world. In His kingdom *dharma* will reign, and there will be no trace of sin; wisdom and bliss will be in one's possession; perfection will be the reward.

For *jñānānandamahauṣadhiḥ*, there is an alternative reading: *jñānānantyamahauṣadhiḥ*.

40

धीयन्त्रेण वचोघटेन कविताकुल्योपकुल्याक्रमै-
रानीतैश्च सदाशिवस्य चरिताम्भोराशिदिव्यामृतैः ।
हृत्केदारयुताश्च भक्तिकलमाः साफल्यमातन्वते
दुर्भिक्षान्मम सेवकस्य भगवन्विश्वेश भीतिः कुतः ॥

dhīyantreṇa vacoghaṭena kavitā kulyopakulyākramair-
ānītaiśca sadāśivasya caritāmbhorāśidivyāmṛtaiḥ|
hṛtkedārayutāśca bhaktikalamāḥ sāphalyam ātanvate
durbhikṣān mama sevakasya bhagavan viśveśa bhītiḥ kutaḥ||

O God ! O Lord of the universe ! With the immortal waters of the story of Sadāśiva, brought with the help of the intellect as water-wheel, speech as vessel, and poesy as channels and subchannels in sequence, the crops of devotion in the fields of the heart become extensively fruitful. How, then, will there be for me, Thy servant, the fear of famine?

Here is the parable of agriculture. For soul-culture, the waters are the stories relating to the greatness of Śiva, the water-wheel is the intellect, the bucket is speech, and the channel is poesy. When the heart is irrigated in this manner, there is a rich yield of devotion resulting in release.

41

पापोत्पातविमोचनाय रुचिरैश्वर्याय मृत्युंजय
स्तोत्रध्याननतिप्रदक्षिणसपर्यालोकनाकर्णने ।
जिह्वाचित्तशिरोङ्घ्रिहस्तनयनश्रोत्रैरहं प्रार्थितो
मामाज्ञापय तन्निरूपय मुहुर्मामेव मा मेऽवचः ॥

pāpotpātavimocanāya ruciraiśvaryāya mṛtyuṁjaya
stotra-dhyāna-nati-pradakṣiṇa-saparyālokanākarṇane|
jihvā-citta-śiroṅghri-hasta-nayana-śrotrair ahaṁ prārthito
mām ājñāpaya tannirūpaya muhur mām eva mā me'vacaḥ||

O Conqueror of Death! I am being entreated by my tongue, mind, head, feet, hands, eyes, and ears, for engaging them, respectively, in singing Thy praise, meditation, bowing, circumambulation, worship, beholding and hearing so that the trouble of sin may be removed and the beatitude may be gained. Do order me; show me the way again and again! Do not observe silence with me.

The essence of devotion is to keep all the sense-organs and mind engaged in the service of the Lord. But how should the Lord be served? What are the disciplines? What are the techniques? These the Lord alone should reveal. Even to worship His feet, His grace there should be. Hence, the devotee implores the Lord to show the means and methods of worship, and entreats Him not to remain silent. Śiva in His role as Dakṣiṇāmūrti taught through silence. The devotee confesses that he is not competent, like Sanaka, Sanandana, Sanātana and Sanatkumāra, to understand the language of silence. So, he tells the Lord, "No Dakṣiṇāmūrti business with me? Please open Thy mouth and teach me through words".

42

गाम्भीर्यं परिखापदं घनधृतिः प्राकार उद्यद्गुण-
स्तोमश्चाप्तबलं घनेन्द्रियचयो द्वाराणि देहे स्थितः ।
विद्या वस्तुसमृद्धिरित्यखिलसामग्रीसमेते सदा
दुर्गातिप्रियदेव मामकमनोदुर्गे निवासं कुरु ।।

gāmbhīryaṁ parikhāpadaṁ ghanadhṛtiḥ prākāra udyadguṇa-
stomaścāptabalaṁ ghanendriyacayo dvārāṇi dehe sthitaḥ/
vidyā vastu-samṛddhir ity akhila-sāmagrīsamete sadā
durgātipriya-deva māmakamano-durge nivāsaṁ kuru//

O God, who art fond of inaccessible fortresses (or, Durgā)! Do stay always in the fortress of my mind which has magnificence as its surrounding moats, great courage as ramparts, high qualities as royal armies and is provided with the gateways of sense-organs that are firm in the body, and is endowed with a profusion of provisions consisting of knowledge, and thus is complete with all the necessary appurtenances.

The mind is compared here to a fortress, and the Lord is invited to take His residence there. The Lord is fond of fortresses. He may well reside in the fortress of the mind. There is a pun on the word *durgā*. It means 'fortress,' and is also a name of Pārvatī.

See *Lalitā-sahasranāma*, v. 50 :
durlabhā durgamā durgā duḥkhahantrī sukhapradā|

43

मा गच्छ त्वमितस्ततो गिरिश भो मय्येव वासं कुरु
स्वामिन्नादिकिरात मामकमनः कान्तारसीमान्तरे ।
वर्तन्ते बहुशो मृगा मदजुषो मात्सर्यमोहादय-
स्तान्हत्वा मृगयाविनोदरुचितालाभं च संप्राप्स्यसि ॥

mā gaccha tvam itastato giriśa bho mayyeva vāsaṁ kuru
svāminn-ādikirāta māmakamanaḥ kāntārasīmāntare|
vartante bahuśo mṛgā madajuṣo mātsaryamohādayas
tān hatvā mṛgayāvinodarucitālābhaṁ ca saṁprāpsyasi||

O Mountain-Resident! O Master! O Primeval Hunter! Do Thou not wander here and there (in search of game)! Do reside in me alone. Within the limits of the dense forest of my mind dwell various kinds of infatuated beasts, viz., jealousy, delusion, etc.; killing them, Thou shalt gain the delight of engaging Thyself in wild-game.

The mind is a dense forest replete with wild game. Let Śiva, the Hunter-chief, indulge in His favourite sport of hunting in this rich forest. Thus the mind will be rid of its passions, and Śiva will have the satisfaction of having done a good job.

The *Mahābhārata* tells us that Śiva assumed the role of a hunter in order to test Arjuna's prowess and grant him the *Pāśupata* weapon.

In the *Śrī-rudra* the following expressions are used with reference to Śiva:

namaste astu dhanvane bāhubhyām uta te namaḥ|

Obeisance be to Thy bow; and obeisance be to Thy two arms?

vanānāṁ pataye namaḥ|

Obeisance to the Lord of the forests!

mṛgayugbhyaḥ namo namaḥ|

Obeisance to the hunter of animals!

namaḥ kāṭhyāya ca|

Obeisance to the One who resides in forests full of stones and thorns!

For *vinodarucitālābhaṁ ca*, there is an alternative reading: *vinodam acirād āgatya.*

44

करलग्नमृगः करीन्द्रभङ्गो
घनशार्दूलविखण्डनोऽस्तजन्तुः ।
गिरिशो विशदाकृतिश्च चेतः-
कुहरे पञ्चमुखोऽस्ति मे कुतो भीः ॥

karalagna-mṛgaḥ karīndra-bhaṅgo
ghana-śārdūla-vikhaṇḍano'sta-jantuḥ|
giriśo viśadākṛtiś ca cetaḥ-
kuhare pañcamukho'sti me kuto bhīḥ||

In the cave of my heart dwells the Lord with five faces (lion), the Mountain-Resident, who holds a deer in the hand (which has caught a deer as prey), who killed the Elephant-demon (which can destroy elephants), who destroyed the ferocious Tiger-demon (which can overcome even tigers), who has on him dead animals (which has near it animals which it has killed), and who has a white form (which has a majestic appearance). Whence is there fear for me!

The present verse is in the form of a pun. The expressions apply both to Śiva and lion. Śiva has five faces; so, He is called *Pañcamukha.* The word also means 'lion'.

The mind of the devotee is described as a cave. When the Śiva-lion resides in this cave, the devotee need have no fear at all.

45

छन्दःशाखिशिखान्वितैर्द्विजवरैः संसेविते शाश्वते
सौख्यापादिनि खेदभेदिनि सुधासारैः फलैर्दीपिते ।
चेतःपक्षिशिखामणे त्यज वृथासंचारमन्यैरलं
नित्यं शङ्करपादपद्मयुगलीनीडे विहारं कुरु ॥

chandaḥśākhi-śikhānvitair dvijavaraiḥ saṁsevite śāśvate
saukhyāpādini khedabhedini sudhāsāraiḥ phalair dīpite|
cetaḥpakṣiśikhāmaṇe tyaja vṛthāsañcāramanyair alaṁ
nityaṁ śaṅkarapādapadmayugalīnīḍe vihāraṁ kuru||

O Mind-bird, the beautiful! Rest always in the nest of the lotus-feet of Śaṅkara, which is sought after by the most learned in the sections of Vedānta (the birds sitting on the branches of the tree), which is eternal (enduring), which affords happiness (comfort), which removes sorrow (weariness), and which shines with fruits of felicity (nectarine fruit). Leave off futile wanderings. You have had enough of other pursuits!

The devotee addresses the mind as a bird, and exhorts it to take shelter in the nest of the Lord's feet. Why should it fly about here and there in vain, only to get exhausted and tired? Its security and safety lie in the nest. Let it rest there in peace and joy!

46

आकीर्णे नखराजिकान्तिविभवैरुद्यत्सुधावैभवै-
राधौतेऽपि च पद्मरागललिते हंसव्रजैराश्रिते ।
नित्यं भक्तिवधूगणैश्च रहसि स्वेच्छाविहारं कुरु
स्थित्वा मानसराजहंस गिरिजानाथाङ्घ्रिसौधान्तरे ॥

ākīrṇe nakharāji-kānti-vibhavair udyat-sudhāvaibhavair
ādhaute'pi ca padmarāga-lalite haṁsavrajair āśrite|
nityaṁ bhaktivadhūgaṇaiś ca rahasi svecchāvihāraṁ kuru
sthitvā mānasa-rājahaṁsa girijānāthāṅghrisaudhāntare||

O Mind, the royal swan! Stay in the mansion of the feet of the Mountain-Daughter's Lord, which is lit by the brilliant splendour of all the toe-nails, white-washed with the rays of the waxing moon, made charming with rubies, and resorted to by the swarm of swans (saints)! In privacy, along with the wives of devotion, may you disport yourself as you please!

The bird-analogy is continued in the present verse. Here, the mind becomes the royal swan, and the Lord's feet its stately mansion. Let the mind stay at Śiva's feet and derive all its pleasures therefrom! It is at His feet that the saints and sages revel. The word *haṁsa* means both 'swan' and 'saint' or 'sage'.

47

शंभुध्यानवसन्तसङ्गिनि हृदारामेऽघजीर्णच्छदाः
स्रस्ता भक्तिलताच्छटा विलसिताः पुण्यप्रवालश्रिताः ।
दीप्यन्ते गुणकोरका जपवचःपुष्पाणि सद्वासना
ज्ञानानन्दसुधामरन्दलहरी संवित्फलाभ्युन्नतिः ॥

śaṁbhudhyāna-vasantasaṅgini hṛdārāme'ghajīrṇacchadāḥ
srastū bhaktilatācchaṭā vilasitāḥ puṇyapravālaśritāḥ/
dīpyante guṇakorakā japavacaḥ puṣpāṇi sadvāsanā
jñānānanda-sudhāmaranda-laharī saṁvitphalābhyunnatiḥ//

In the garden of the heart that is in the spring season of meditation on Śaṁbhu, the assemblage of creeper-plants of devotion which have shed the old leaves of sins and taken on the fresh tender leaves of merit, the buds of virtue, the blooms of words that repeat the sacred names, the sweet scents (good impressions), the profusion of the nectar-juice of flowers of wisdom and bliss, the increase of the fruit of consciousness — these abound in a brilliant manner.

Here is a poetic description of the devoted heart. The heart is the delightful garden where the creepers of devotion grow in profusion. The season too is propitious — the spring season of meditation. A rich harvest is assured, of beautiful flowers and delicious fruits — good words, good deeds, and good thoughts.

48

नित्यानन्दरसालयं सुरमुनिस्वान्ताम्बुजाताश्रयं
स्वच्छं सद्द्विजसेवितं कलुषहृत्सद्वासनाविष्कृतम् ।
शंभुध्यानसरोवरं व्रज मनोहंसावतंस स्थिरं
किं क्षुद्राश्रयपल्वलभ्रमणसंजातश्रमं प्राप्स्यसि ॥

nityānanda-rasālayaṁ suramunisvāntāmbujātāśrayaṁ
svacchaṁ sad-dvija-sevitaṁ kaluṣa-hṛt sadvāsanāviṣkṛtam/
śaṁbhudhyāna-sarovaraṁ vraja manohaṁsāvataṁsa sthiraṁ
kiṁ kṣudrāśraya-palvala-bhramaṇasaṁjātāśramaṁ prāpsyasi.

O Mind, the best of swans! Go to the lake of the meditation on Śaṁbhu, which is the reservoir of eternal bliss, which blooms with the lotuses of the hearts of gods and ascetics, which is clear and is resorted to by the good and the wise (swans), which removes dirt (sin), which emits good scents, and which is calm. Why do you tire yourself by wandering in the muddy pools of service to the low?

Here again the mind is addressed as the royal swan. Its proper place is in the limpid lake of Śiva-meditation. Let it not demean itself by resorting to muddy pools — the so-called patrons who are small-minded and hard-hearted!

There is deprecation, once again, of the seeking of patronage under people who are low and mean.

49

आनन्दामृतपूरिता हरपदाम्भोजालवालोद्यता
स्थैर्योपघ्नमुपेत्य भक्तिलतिका शाखोपशाखान्विता ।
उच्चैर्मानसकायमानपटलीमाक्रम्य निष्कल्मषा
नित्याभीष्टफलप्रदा भवतु मे सत्कर्मसंवर्धिता ॥

ānandāmṛtapūritā harapadāmbhojālavālodyatā
sthairyopaghnam upetya bhaktilatikā śākhopaśākhānvitā|
uccairmānasakāyamānapaṭalīm ākramya niṣkalmaṣā
nityābhīṣṭaphalapradā bhavatu me satkarmasaṁvardhitā||

May the creeper of devotion yield me the fruit that I always desire — the creeper that has been nurtured by the water of joy, that has sprouted and grown from the lotus-feet of Śiva, that is rich with shoots and sub-shoots, having entwined itself around a supporting pole (constancy or firmness), that has spread itself over the lofty mind-*pandal*, that is without blemishes, and that has been nourished with good deeds!

In verse 47, devotion was compared to creepers. Here, the process whereby the devotion-creeper could be nurtured and made to yield the maximum fruit is described. Let the waters of divine ecstasy nourish it. Let it sprout from the feet of the Lord. Let it be supported by the characteristics of constancy. Let it spread all over the mind and cover it. Thus will pure devotion, augmented by good deeds, yield the fruit of true wisdom leading to release.

50

संध्यारम्भविजृम्भितं श्रुतिशिरःस्थानान्तराधिष्ठितं
सप्रेमभ्रमराभिराममसकृत्सद्वासनाशोभितम् ।
भोगीन्द्राभरणं समस्तसुमनःपूज्यं गुणाविष्कृतं
सेवे श्रीगिरिमल्लिकार्जुनमहालिङ्गं शिवालिङ्गितम् ॥

sandhyārambha-vijṛmbhitaṁ śrutiśiraḥ sthānāntar-ādhiṣṭhitaṁ
saprema-bhramarābhirāmam asakṛt-sadvāsanāśobhitam|
bhogīndrābharaṇaṁ samastasumanaḥpūjyaṁ guṇāviṣkṛtaṁ
seve śrīgiri-mallikārjuna-mahāliṅgaṁ śivāliṅgitam||

I adore Mallikārjuna, the great Liṅga at Śrī-Śaila (the Arjuna tree entwined by jasmine creepers on the beautiful mountain), who is embraced by Pārvatī (which is auspicious), who dances wonderfully at dusk (which blooms profusely in the evening), who is established through Vedānta (whose flowers are placed on one's ears and head), who is pleasing with the loving Bhramarāmbikā by His side (which is grand with eager honey-bees humming around), who shines in the repeated contemplations of pious people (which always wafts good scent), who wears serpents as ornaments (which embellishes those who seek enjoyment), who is worshipped by all the gods (which is the best of flower-trees), and who expresses virtue (and which is well-known for its high quality).

In this verse and the next is celebrated the Śiva-liṅga of Śrī-śaila. Śrī-śaila in Āndhra is a renowned place of Śaiva pilgrimage. The Liṅga of this holy place bears the name 'Mallikārjuna'; and the Devī is known by the name 'Bhramarāmbikā'. The term 'Arjuna' is also the name of a tree. And, 'Bhramarāmbikā' may mean also the female-bee. Hence, there is a pun on the words of this verse.

51

भृङ्गीच्छानटनोत्कटः करिमदग्राही स्फुरन्माधवा-
ह्लादो नादयुतो महासितवपुः पञ्चेषुणा चादृतः ।
सत्पक्षः सुमनोवनेषु स पुनः साक्षान्मदीये मनो-
राजीवे भ्रमराधिपो विहरतां श्रीशैलवासी विभुः ॥

bhṛṅgīcchānaṭanotkaṭaḥ karimadagrāhī sphuranmādhavā-
hlādo nādayuto mahāsitavapuḥ pañceṣuṇā cādṛtaḥ|
satpakṣaḥ sumanovaneṣu sa punaḥ sākṣānmadīye mano-
rājīve bhramarādhipo viharatāṁ śrīśailavāsī vibhuḥ||

The all-pervading Lord of Bhramarāṁbikā who resides in Śrī-Saila (the bee that resides on the hill and goes about everywhere), who dances in accordance with the wish of sage Bhṛṅgin (which follows the lead of the queen-bee), who quelled the pride of the Elephant-demon (which drinks the rut of elephants), who is delightful with the effulgent Mahāviṣṇu (which delights in the spring season), who is endowed with the sound 'Om' (which makes the ringing sound), who has a shining body (which has blue-black body), who is the refuge of Manmatha (which is an accomplice of the god of love), who is intent on protecting the good (which is found in the flower gardens, and has beautiful wings), and who is immediately present (which is before one's eyes)—may He revel in my mind-lotus !

Here again is a pun on the words. The references are to the Lord of Śrī-śaila and to the chief bee.

Mallikārjuna Mahāliṅga is one of the twelve Jyotirliṅgas, the most sacred of Śiva's emblems. The twelve Liṅgas are these: (1) Somanātha in Saurāṣṭra, (2) Mallikārjuna at Śrī-śaila, (3) Mahākāla at Ujjayinī, (4) Parameṣvara at Oṁkāra, (5) Kedāra on the Himālayas, (6) Bhīmaśaṅkara at Ḍākinī, (7) Viśveśa at Vārāṇasī, (8) Tryambaka at the source of the Godāvarī, (9) Vaidyanātha at Citābhūmi, (10) Nāgeśa at Dārukāvana. (11) Rāmeśa at Setubandha, and (12) Ghuśmeśa at Śivālaya. The very utterance of the names of these Liṅgas is believed to confer on the devotee great merit and all that is auspicious.

52

कारुण्यामृतवर्षिणं घनविपद्ग्रीष्मच्छिदाकर्मठं
विद्यासस्यफलोदयाय सुमनःसंसेव्यमिच्छाकृतिम् ।
नृत्यद्भक्तमयूरमद्रिनिलयं चञ्चज्जटामण्डलं
शंभो वाञ्छति नीलकंधर सदा त्वां मे मनश्चातकः ॥

kāruṇyāmṛtavarṣiṇaṁ ghanavipadgrīṣmacchidākarmaṭhaṁ
vidyāsasyaphalodayāya sumanaḥ- saṁsevyam icchākṛtim|
nṛtyad-bhaktamayūram adrinilayaṁ cañcajjaṭāmaṇḍalaṁ
śaṁbho vāñchati nīlakaṁdhara sadā tvāṁ me manaścātakaḥ||

O Giver of auspiciousness ! O blue-throated Lord! (O dark water-cloud!) The cātaka bird of my mind always longs for Thee who dost shower the ambrosia of compassion (the cloud which pours down merciful water), who hast the power to remove formidable difficulties (which is capable of removing burning heat), who art adored by the pious for the sake of gaining the fruit of wisdom (which is desired by good farmers for cultivating plentiful crops), who canst take any form (which assumes odd shapes), who art surrounded by dancing devotees (which is pleasing to the dancing peacocks), who livest on the mountain (which is over the peaks of hill), and who hast moving matted locks (and which is accompanied by brilliant lightning).

There is a pun in this verse also. The references are to Śiva and the rain-cloud. The term *Nīlakaṁdhara* means (1) the Blue-throated Lord, and (2) the rain-bearing cloud. Cātaka is a bird which depends for its sustenance on the rain-drops directly as they fall. Hence, its intense longing for the rain-clouds. "Similarly", says the devotee, "does my mind pant for Thee, O Lord!". At the sight of the rain-cloud, the peacocks spread their plumage and dance in glee. So do the devotees dance in joy at the vision of the Lord. The gentle rain that falls from above removes the bad effects of heat, makes the soil fertile, and provides sustenance for all beings. Śiva, the supreme Lord, destroys all sorrow and grants the final beatitude to the soul, through the grace that flows out of Him.

53

आकाशेन शिखी समस्तफणिनां नेत्रा कलापी नता-
नुग्राहिप्रणवोपदेशनिनदैः केकीति यो गीयते ।
श्यामां शैलसमुद्भवां घनरुचिं दृष्ट्वा नटन्तं मुदा
वेदान्तोपवने विहाररसिकं तं नीलकण्ठं भजे ॥

ākāśena śikhī samasta-phaṇināṁ netrā kalāpī natā-
nugrāhi-praṇavopadeśaninadaiḥ kekīti yo gīyate|
śyāmāṁ śailasamudbhavāṁ ghanarucim dṛṣṭvā naṭantaṁ mudā
vedāntopavane vihārarasikaṁ taṁ nīlakaṇṭhaṁ bhaje||

I adore the blue-throated Lord (peacock) who has the sky as his crest, who wears the chief of all the serpents as ornament, who is praised as being endowed with 'kekī' sounds by the utterances of instruction in the syllable 'Om' which blesses the devotees, who dances in mirth seeing Pārvatī, daughter of the Mountain, bearing a sheen like the cloud, and who enjoys sporting in the forest of Vedānta.

In this and the next few verses, the dancing form of Śiva is praised. In the present verse, the Lord is likened unto a peacock. For this cosmic Peacock, the sky is the crest, the peahen is Pārvatī, and the dance-ground is Vedānta. Serpents are Its ornaments, and the Praṇava is Its sound-symbol.

The term *Nīlakaṇṭha* is here used to mean (1) Śiva with blue throat, and (2) the peacock with blue coloured neck.

54

संध्या घर्मदिनात्ययो हरिकराघातप्रभूतानक-
ध्वानो वारिदगर्जितं दिविषदां दृष्टिच्छटा चञ्चला ।
भक्तानां परितोषबाष्पविततिर्वृष्टिर्मयूरी शिवा
यस्मिन्नुज्ज्वलताण्डवं विजयते तं नीलकण्ठं भजे ॥

sandhyā gharmadinātyayo harikarāghātaprabhūtānaka-
dhvāno vāridagarjitaṁ diviṣadāṁ dṛṣṭicchaṭā cañcalā|
bhaktānāṁ paritoṣabāṣpavitatir vṛṣṭir mayūrī śivā
yasminn ujjvala-tāṇḍavaṁ vijayate taṁ nīlakaṇṭhaṁ bhaje||

I adore the blue-throated Lord (peacock) whose scintillating dance prevails, with the evening as the end of the summer season, with the sound produced by the beating of the drum by Viṣṇu as the rumbling of the clouds, with the row of eyes of the heavenly gods as lightning shafts, with the tears of joy shed by the devotees as rain, and with Pārvatī as peahen.

Here is a description of the glorious dance of the Lord in the evening. The simile of the peacock is continued. For the peacock's dance, the accompaniments are the thunder-cloud, lightning shafts, shower of rain, and peahen. For the Lord's cosmic dance, the accompaniments are the drum-beat by Viṣṇu, the sparkling eyes of the gods that witness the dance in wonderment, the joyous tears of devotees, and the Lady of the Mountain, Pārvatī.

55

आद्यायामिततेजसे श्रुतिपदैर्वेद्याय साध्याय ते
विद्यानन्दमयात्मने त्रिजगतः संरक्षणोद्योगिने ।
ध्येयायाखिलयोगिभिः सुरगणैर्गेयाय मायाविने
सम्यक्ताण्डवसंभ्रमाय जटिने सेयं नतिः शंभवे ॥

ādyāyāmita-tejase śrutipadair vedyāya sādhyāya te
vidyānandamayātmane trijagataḥ saṁrakṣaṇodyogine|
dhyeyāyākhilayogibhiḥ suragaṇair geyāya māyāvine
samyak tāṇḍava-saṁbhramāya jaṭine seyaṁ natiḥ śaṁbhave||

May this obeisance be to Thee, Śaṁbhu with the matted locks, who art the first cause, the limitless light, who art known through the texts of Scripture, who art what is to be gained, of the nature of knowledge and bliss, who art intent on saving the three worlds, who art the object of meditation for all the *yogins*, and whose praise is sung by the groups of gods, who art the wielder of *māyā*, and who art engaged in dancing exquisitely.

It is from the dance of Śaṁbhu that the universe arises; it is by that dance that the universe is sustained; and it is through the divine dance that the universe is dissolved. It is dance that veils the truth, and it is dance that showers grace upon the soul. The five functions of Śiva are but different forms of His dance. The five functions are: creation (*sṛṣṭi*), preservation (*sthiti*), destruction (*saṁhāra*), veiling (*tirodhāna*), and bestowing grace (*anugraha*). The dance is Śiva's (*māyā*). Hence, He is called *māyāvin*. Śiva is the ground of all beings, the source of all things. He is of the nature of existence (*sat*), consciousness (*cit*), bliss (*ānanda*). He is known through the Vedas. He is the supreme goal. He is the one support of all the worlds. It is on Him that the yogins meditate; it is His praise that the gods sing. Wonderful is His cosmic dance—the dance that sustains and saves all beings!

56

नित्याय त्रिगुणात्मने पुरजिते कात्यायनीश्रेयसे
सत्यायादिकुटुम्बिने मुनिमनः प्रत्यक्षचिन्मूर्तये ।
मायासृष्टजगत्त्रयाय सकलाम्नायान्तसंचारिणे
सायंताण्डवसंभ्रमाय जटिने सेयं नतिः शंभवे ॥

nityāya triguṇātmane purajite kātyāyanīśreyase
satyāyādikuṭumbine munimanaḥ-pratyakṣacinmūrtaye/
māyāsṛṣṭa-jagattrayāya sakalāmnāyāntasaṁcāriṇe
sāyaṁ-tāṇḍava-saṁbhramāya jaṭine seyaṁ natiḥ śaṁbhave//

May this obeisance be to Thee, Śaṁbhu with the matted locks, who art eternal, who art embodied in the three *guṇas*, who didst conquer the cities, who art the supreme value for Pārvatī, the truth, the first *pater familias*, who art of the nature of consciousness directly perceived by the ascetics in their minds; who didst create the three worlds through *māyā*, who dost move in all the Vedānta texts, and who art engaged in dancing the evening dance.

Here, again, we have a glorious vision of Śiva's evening-dance. It is the Eternal that dances—the great Lord with matted locks, indicating the cardinal directions in space. It is with Pārvatī by His side that He dances, and thus creates the world through *māyā*. His is the first family (*ādikuṭumba*). As a familiar verse says:

mātā ca pārvatī devī pitā devo maheśvaraḥ.

(Pārvatī is the Mother, and Maheśvara is the Father).

Although He is omnipresent and is the source of all beings and their first parent, it is not easy to realize Him. He becomes manifest only to the sages and saints. And, He is knowable through Vedānta alone.

57

नित्यं स्वोदरपूरणाय सकलानुद्दिश्य वित्ताशया
व्यर्थं पर्यटनं करोमि भवतः सेवां न जाने विभो ।
मज्जन्मान्तरपुण्यपाकबलतस्त्वं शर्व सर्वान्तर-
स्तिष्ठस्येव हि तेन वा पशुपते ते रक्षणीयोऽस्म्यहम् ॥

nityaṁ svodara-pūraṇāya sakalān uddiśya vittāśayā
vyarthaṁ paryaṭanaṁ karomi bhavataḥ sevāṁ na jāne vibho|
majjanmāntara-puṇyapāka-balatas tvaṁ śarva sarvāntaras
tiṣṭhasyeva hi tena vā paśupate te rakṣaṇīyo'smy aham||

O Lord of souls, O the all-pervading One!, O Śiva! I seek all people always, motivated by desire for wealth and for the sake of filling my belly, and thus wander in vain; and to be in Thy service I do not know. On the strength of the maturation of the merit acquired by me in previous lives, Thou stayest as the inner ruler of all. Therefore it is but meet that I should be protected by Thee.

The futility of seeking the patronage of low people by serving them is pointed out more than once in this poem. Even if such people extend their patronage, it is not good. Such patronage blesses neither those who give nor those who receive. Yet, the average individual, prompted by greed for wealth dances attendance on those whom he considers to be rich and powerful, on account of delusion. What a waste of time, and what misuse of God-given opportunity !

In spite of this, some souls feel the presence of God on account of past merit. The way to perfection lies open before them. If they take to the way, they will be saved.

58

एको वारिजबान्धवः क्षितिनभोव्याप्तं तमोमण्डलं
भित्वा लोचनगोचरोऽपि भवति त्वं कोटिसूर्यप्रभः ।
वेद्यः किं न भवस्यहो घनतरं कीदृग्भवेन्मत्तम-
स्तत्सर्वं व्यपनीय मे पशुपते साक्षात्प्रसन्नो भव ॥

eko vārija-bāndhavaḥ kṣitinabhovyāptaṁ tamomaṇḍalaṁ
bhittvā locanagocaro'pi bhavati tvaṁ koṭisūryaprabhaḥ/
vedyaḥ kiṁ na bhavasyaho ghanataraṁ kīdṛgbhaven-mattamas
tat-sarvaṁ vyapanīya me paśupate sākṣāt prasanno bhava//

O Lord of souls! The one sun, destroying the darkness that pervades earth and heaven, becomes visible. Thy luminosity exceeds that of crores of suns! Why, then, does not Thou become known? Oh, how intensely dense my darkness (ignorance) should be? Do destroy this entirely, and become directly manifest to me.

The supreme Self is self-luminous. It does not require any other light for becoming manifest. In the physical world, the sun is a luminary that shines by itself. In the spiritual sense, the Self has transcendent luminosity. If we must use a physical imagery, we must say that the luminosity of the Self exceeds that of a crore of suns. Yet, why is it not manifest to us ? It is not true to say that the Self is not manifest at all. The Self is not fully manifest either. It is manifest, and yet not manifest. (See *Pañcadaśī*, i. 11: *bhāne'py abhātāsau.*) This paradoxical situation is the result of *māyā* or *avidyā* (nescience). The devotee appeals to the supreme Self, God, for effecting the removal of nescience.

59

हंसः पद्मवनं समिच्छति यथा नीलाम्बुदं चातकः
कोकः कोकनदप्रियं प्रतिदिनं चन्द्रं चकोरस्तथा ।
चेतो वाञ्छति मामकं पशुपते चिन्मार्गमृग्यं विभो
गौरीनाथ भवत्पदाब्जयुगलं कैवल्यसौख्यप्रदम् ॥

haṁsaḥ padmavanaṁ samicchati yathā nīlāmbudaṁ cātakaḥ
kokaḥ kokanadapriyaṁ pratidinaṁ candraṁ cakoras tathā|
ceto vāñchati māmakaṁ paśupate cinmārgamṛgyaṁ vibho
gaurīnātha bhavat-padābja-yugalaṁ kaivalya-saukhya-pradam||

O Lord of souls! O, the all-pervading One! O Consort of Pārvatī! Just as the swan longs for the lotus-tank, the cātaka bird for the dark rain-clouds, the cakravāka bird for the sun, and the cakora bird for the moon, so does my mind long for Thy lotus-feet which are to be reached through the path of knowledge, and which yield the bliss of perfection.

Some similes are given here for the longing of the devotee's heart for God. In each of the pairs mentioned, the lower member cannot do without the higher member; it is dependent on, and is devoted to the other. The pairs are these: the swan and the louts-tank, the cātaka bird and the rain-cloud, the cakravāka bird and the sun, the cakora bird and the moon. Here, we have four species of birds; each longs for the member mentioned along with it. The swan subsists on the lotus-stalks. The cātaka bird, as we have already seen, is said to live by drinking rain-drops. The cakravāka couples, it is believed, are separated and mourn during night; hence, their longing for the sun. The cakora bird is supposed to subsist on moon-beams. Likewise is the devotee's heart on the feet of the Lord.

60

रोधस्तोयहृतः श्रमेण पथिकश्छायां तरोर्वृष्टितो
भीतः स्वस्थगृहं गृहस्थमतिथिर्दीनः प्रभुं धार्मिकम् ।

दीपं संतमसाकुलश्च शिखिनं शीताव़ृतस्त्वं तथा
चेत: सर्वभयापहं व्रज सुखं शम्भो: पदाम्भोरुहम् ॥

rodhastoyahṛtaḥ śrameṇa pathikaś chāyāṁ taror-vṛṣṭito
bhītaḥ svasthagṛhaṁ gṛhasthaṁ atithir dīnaḥ prabhuṁ
dhārmikam/
dīpaṁ saṁtamasākulaś ca śikhinaṁ śītāvṛtastvaṁ tathā
cetaḥ sarvabhayāpahaṁ vraja sukhaṁ śambhoḥ
padāmbhoruham//

Just as a man being dragged by a current of
water seeks to reach the shore, a tired traveller
the shade of a tree, the one afraid of rain the
shelter of his house, a guest the house-holder,
the one who is poor the philanthropic gentleman, the one who is troubled by dense darkness
a lamp, and the one who is afflicted by cold,
fire, even so, O mind, reach with ease the lotus-
feet of Śaṁbhu that can drive away all fear!

Some more similes, to explain the need for the soul to seek
shelter at the feet of the Lord. In each of the pairs, there is
the relation of the protected and protector, the sheltered and
shelter, the saved and saviour. There are bitter situations from
which one may want to be saved; in each case, one longs for
that which will save him. A person caught in a rushing stream
will find safety if he manages to reach the shore. A weary
traveller will be on the look-out for the shade of a tree. A man
drenched in rain will want to take shelter in a house. A
mendicant will go to a house-holder for alms. A poor man will
seek the patronage of a rich person who is generous. The one
who gropes in the dark will badly need a lamp. A person in
freezing cold will endeavour to reach a fireside. Similarly, the
one who wants to gain freedom from fear should take refuge
in the Lord. And, who is there that does not want to get rid of
fear ?

61

अङ्कोलं निजबीजसंततिरयस्कान्तोपलं सूचिका
साध्वी नैजविभुं लता क्षितिरुहं सिन्धुः सरिद्वल्लभम् ।
प्राप्नोतीह यथा तथा पशुपतेः पादारविन्दद्वयं
चेतोवृत्तिरुपेत्य तिष्ठति सदा सा भक्तिरित्युच्यते ॥

aṅkolaṁ nija-bīja-santatir ayaskāntopalaṁ sūcikā
sādhvī naija-vibhuṁ latā kṣitiruhaṁ sindhuḥ saridvallabham|
prāpnotīha yathā tathā paśupateḥ pādāravindadvayaṁ
cetovṛttir upetya tiṣṭhati sadā sā bhaktir ity ucyate||

Just as, here, the seeds of the *aṅkola* tree go and attach themselves to the tree, the needle sticks to the magnet, the chaste woman to her lord, the creeper to the tree, and the river (runs) to the ocean, even so if the flow of the mind reaches the lotus-feet of the Lord of souls and remains there always, that is called devotion.

The previous two verses lead to the present one where devotion is defined. The similes given here are taken from the living as well as non-living realms. Here, again, the higher member of each pair is indispensable for the lower member. These similes are meant to illustrate the nature and value of constant attachment to a single ideal. Such constancy, when it is in relation to God, is called devotion (*bhakti*).

62

आनन्दाश्रुभिरातनोति पुलकं नैर्मल्यतश्छादनं
वाचाशङ्खमुखे स्थितैश्च जठरापूर्ति चरित्रामृतैः ।
रुद्राक्षैर्भसितेन देव वपुषो रक्षां भवद्भावना-
पर्यङ्के विनिवेश्य भक्तिजननी भक्तार्भकं रक्षति ॥

ānandāśrubhir ātanoti pulakaṁ nairmalyataśchādanaṁ
vācāśaṅkhamukhe sthitaiśca jaṭharāpūrtiṁ caritrāmṛtaiḥ|
rudrākṣair bhasitena deva vapuṣo rakṣāṁ bhavad-bhāvanā-
paryaṅke viniveśya bhaktijananī bhaktārbhakaṁ rakṣati||

O God! The mother, Devotion, protects the child, the devotee, by bathing (thrilling) him in (with) the waters (tears) of bliss, by dressing him in the clothes of purity, by feeding him with the ambrosia of Thy stories contained in the mouth of the conch, the speech, by girding his body with the amulets of Rudra-beads and sacred ash, and by putting him to sleep in the cradle of Thy contemplation.

Devotion is, here, compared to a mother, and the devotee to her child. Devotion invests the devotee with both external indications and internal characteristics of God-love. Rudrākṣa-beads and sacred ash adorn his body. He relates the legends about Śiva, and enjoys listening to them when related by fellow-devotees. Tears of joy flow from his eyes. His mind becomes pure. And, he loses himself in divine contemplation.

Of the devotees, the *Nāradabhakti-sūtra* (68) says: 'Conversing with one another with voice choked, eyes shedding joyful tears, and body thrilled, they purify their families and the entire earth.'

63

मार्गावर्तितपादुका पशुपतेरङ्गस्य कूर्चायते
गण्डूषाम्बुनिषेचनं पुररिपोर्दिव्याभिषेकायते ।
किंचिद्भक्षितमांसशेषकवलं नव्योपहारायते
भक्तिः किं न करोत्यहो वनचरो भक्तावतंसायते ॥

mārgāvartita-pādukā paśupater aṅgasya kūrcāyate
gaṇḍūṣāmbu-niṣecanaṁ puraripor divyābhiṣekāyate/
kiṁcid-bhakṣita-māṁsaśeṣakavalaṁ navyopahārāyate
bhaktiḥ kiṁ na karoty aho vanacaro bhaktāvataṁsāyate//

The foot-wear worn out through use on (forest) paths became the indicator betwixt the eye-brows on the body of the Lord of souls; the pouring of water borne in the mouth became divine bath for the Conqueror of the Cities; the remnant handful of meat, part of which had been eaten, became fresh food-offering. What will not devotion do? Ah, the hunter became the best of devotees!

Here is Śaṅkara's tribute to Kaṇṇappar as the paragon of devotees. The wild hunter worshipped the Lord in his own bizarre way. He did not know the *śāstras*. The rules of formal worship were unknown to him. Of the need for external purity while offering worship, he had not even an inkling. His strange mode of worship was regarded as an act of desecration by the temple-priest. But it was that worship that pleased the Lord most. The hunter received the name 'Kaṇṇappar' from the Lord, because he had given one eye to Him and was ready to give the other one also. Who can excel Kaṇṇappar in devotion? He was, indeed, the foremost among *bhaktas*.

Māṇikkavācakar has the following verse in his *Tiruvācakam* (G. U. Pope's translation):

'There was no love in me like Kaṇṇappan's:
　When He, my Sire, saw this, me poor
Beyond compare, in grace He made His own;
　He spake, and bade me come to Him.
With heavenly grace adorned He shines, and wears
　White ashes, and the golden dust!
To Him,—of mercy infinite,—go thou,
　And breathe His praise, O humming bee'.
(*Tirukkōttumbi*. 4.)

Schomerus observes: "In the Periapurāṇa it is related of Kaṇṇappan that while out shooting he found an abandoned statue of Śiva and forgetting the world and himself out of love towards Śiva he put himself entirely to the service of the Śiva statue and even sacrificed his eyes in the service." (Quoted by Soderblom in *Living God*, O.U.P., 1933, pp. 137-8).

64

वक्षस्ताडनमन्तकस्य कठिनापस्मारसंमर्दनं
भूभृत्पर्यटनं नमत्सुरशिरःकोटीरसंघर्षणम् ।
कर्मेदं मृदुलस्य तावकपदद्वन्द्वस्य किं वोचितं
मच्चेतोमणिपादुकाविहरणं शम्भो सदाङ्गीकुरु ॥

vakṣastāḍanam antakasya kaṭhināpasmārasaṁmardanaṁ
bhūbhṛt-paryaṭanaṁ namat-suraśiraḥ-koṭīra-saṁgharṣaṇam|
karmedaṁ mṛdulasya tāvaka-pada-dvandvasya kiṁ vocitaṁ
macceto-maṇipādukā-viharaṇaṁ śambho sadāṅgīkuru||

O Śaṁbhu! Kicking at the chest of Yama, destruction of the hard Apasmāra (nescience), roaming about on Kailāsa Mount, rubbing against the crowns worn by the gods on their bowed heads—these constitute the work of Thy tender feet. But is this proper? Do agree to go about wearing the jewelled foot-wear of my mind.

The devotee offers his mind as footwear to the Lord. Śiva has to perform very hard tasks with His feet. Without proper protection for His feet, He should not undertake these tasks.

Let us consider some of the tough functions the Lord assigns to His feet:—

(1) Mārkaṇḍeya was destined to live only for sixteen years. When the appointed time drew near, his parents became depressed and disconsolate. The boy assured them that he would conquer death. He went into the temple and gave himself up to the worship of Śiva-liṅga. Yama, the god of death, sent his emissaries to fetch Mārkaṇḍeya's life. But they could not approach the *sanctum sanctorum* where the boy was worshipping Śiva. Then, Yama himself came. The Lord arose out of the Liṅga and kicked Yama at the chest. Yama died and was revived by the Lord through His grace. Mārkaṇḍeya conquered death and became a *cirajīvin*.

Kicking at Yama's chest with the bare foot was hard work, indeed, by our standards. It is interesting to note that Saint Sundarar characterises it as a terrible deed, *udaitta koduṁ toḷil* (7, 61, 4).

(2) One of the creatures that came out of the Dārukavana sacrifice was the *Apasmāra*, a malignant epileptic dwarf. Like his predecessors, he had a go at Śiva, but only to be crushed. With the tip of His foot, Śiva pressed the Apasmāra's back and broke it. In the figure of the dancing Śiva, Naṭarāja, the Apasmāra is represented as lying under the feet of the Lord.

The term *apasmāra* means the epileptic fit which drives the patient out of normal consciousness and gives him an accession of strength. Its Tamil equivalent is *muyalakan*. The *Apasmāra* symbolises nescience, the primal cause of bondage. Since it is hard to be removed, the epithet *kaṭhina* is given to it in the present verse.

(3) The Mount Kailāsa is Śiva's place of residence. His feet have to constantly tread the hard rocks.

(4) The gods vie with one another in bowing at the feet of the Lord. In their enthusiasm to show reverence, they forget that they are causing the Lord considerable inconvenience, from our standpoint, by rubbing against His feet with their crowned heads. (See v. 17).

The Lord's feet have to perform such hard tasks constantly. The devotee offers the Lord his mind as foot-wear, which is good and beautiful, and fit to be worn by Him.

For *kiṁ vocitam*, an alternative reading: *gaurīpate*.

65

वक्षस्ताडनशङ्कया विचलितो वैवस्वतो निर्जराः
कोटीरोज्ज्वलरत्नदीपकलिकानीराजनं कुर्वते ।
दृष्ट्वा मुक्तिवधूस्तनोति निभृताश्लेषं भवानीपते
यच्चेतस्तव पादपद्मभजनं तस्येह किं दुर्लभम् ॥

vakṣastāḍana-śaṅkayā vicalito vaivasvato nirjarāḥ
koṭīrojjvala-ratnadīpakalikā-nīrājanaṁ kurvate|
dṛṣṭvā muktivadhūs tanoti nibhṛtāśleṣaṁ bhavānīpate
yaccetas tava pādapadma-bhajanaṁ tasyeha kiṁ durlabham||

O Consort of Pārvatī! What is impossible for him, here, whose mind worships Thy Feet? Seeing him, Yama runs away, fearing another kick at the chest; the gods wave the lamps consisting of the flaming gems that are set in their crowns; and the Mukti bride (Release) holds him in inseparable embrace.

Mārkaṇḍeya's was not the only instance of a devotee conquering death. Every devotee of God realizes deathlessness. The status of the devotee is far superior even to that of the gods, the so-called immortals. The gods adore the devotee, for in doing so they know that they are adoring Śiva. When they pass before the devotee with bowed heads wearing bejewelled crowns, it appears like a row of lamps being waved ceremonially in worship. The fruit of *mokṣa* is what the devotee reaps through his devotion to Śiva.

66

क्रीडार्थं सृजसि प्रपञ्चमखिलं क्रीडामृगास्ते जना
यत्कर्माचरितं मया च भवतः प्रीत्यै भवत्येव तत् ।
शम्भो स्वस्य कुतूहलस्य करणं मच्चेष्टितं निश्चितं
तस्मान्मामकरक्षणं पशुपते कर्तव्यमेव त्वया ॥

krīḍārthaṁ sṛjasi prapañcam akhilaṁ krīḍāmṛgās te janā
yat-karmācaritaṁ mayā ca bhavataḥ prītyai bhavaty eva tat|
śambho svasya kutūhalasya karaṇaṁ maccesṭitaṁ niścitaṁ
tasmān māmakarakṣaṇaṁ paśupate kartavyam eva tvayā||

O Śaṁbhu! Thou createst the entire universe in sport; the people (in it) are Thy game. Whatever deed is performed by me—that is for Thy pleasure alone. Hence it is certain that my deeds are only for Thy exaltation, O Lord of souls! my protection, therefore, is Thy concern.

God creates the world in sport. When it is said that creation is God's sport, what is meant is this: the creation is effortless; God does not create the world, as a potter produces a pot; nor is creation comparable to the transformation of milk into curds. Creation is effortless in the sense that it is a transfiguration (*vivarta*). Secondly, God does not create the world with any selfish motive. He has no purpose of His own to gain. As the *Gītā* puts it, there is nothing unaccomplished for Him, nor is there anything to be accomplished (*nānavāptaṁ avāptavyam.* iii, 22).

Brahma-sūtra, II, i, 33, declares: *lokavat tu līlākaivalyam.* But (Brahman's creative activity) is mere sport, such as we see in the empirical world. In his commentary on this *sūtra*, Śaṅkara observes that God's creative activity is like the doings of princes or ministers which have no reference to any extraneous purpose, but are expressions of mere sportfulness. The creative act is comparable to the process of normal breathing, which is effortless and has no extraneous purpose. In the sport-activities of men, it may be possible at least to detect some subtle or hidden motive. In the case of God's creative activity, even this is not possible. And, it must be remembered that the creation-texts of Scripture refer to the nescience-posited name- and form-world.

If creation is God's sport, then the world's denizens must be considered to be His game. All that these beings do should be regarded as willed by Him alone. The devotee realizes this truth and dedicates all his activities to God.

yad-yad-karma karomi tattadakhilam śaṁbho tavārādhanam.
"What act I do perform,
O Śaṁbhu, may that be dedicated to Thee!"

67

बहुविधपरितोषबाष्पपूर-
स्फुटपुलकाङ्कितचारुभोगभूमिम् ।
चिरपदफलकाङ्क्षिसेव्यमानां
परमसदाशिवभावनां प्रपद्ये ॥

bahuvidha-paritoṣa-bāṣpapūra-
sphuṭa-pulakāṅkita-cārubhoga-bhūmim|
cirapada-phalakāṅkṣi-sevyamānāṁ
paramasadāśiva-bhāvanāṁ prapadye||

I seek refuge in the contemplation of the supreme Sadāśiva, which is the pretty land of enjoyment characterized by tears of joy and thrills of body engendered by various delights, and which is adorned by those who desire the fruit consisting of the status eternal.

Meditation on Śiva is compared to a rich and fruitful field of enjoyment. What one obtains from this field is emancipation.

68

अमितमुदमृतं मुहुर्दुहन्तीं
विमलभवत्पदगोष्ठमावसन्तीम् ।
सदय पशुपते सुपुण्यपाकां
मम परिपालय भक्तिधेनुमेकाम् ॥

amitamudamṛtaṁ muhurduhantīṁ
vimalabhavatpada-goṣṭham-āvasantīm|
sadaya paśupate supuṇyapākāṁ
mama paripālaya bhaktidhenumekām||

O Lord of souls; O Compassionate One! Please protect this single cow of mine, Devotion, which is the fruit of meritorious deeds, which yields repeatedly and plentifully the delight—giving milk, and which resides in the cow-pen of Thy blemishless Feet.

Devotion is, here, described to be a blemishless cow that deserves to be protected by the Lord. Devotion is the spiritual *kāmadhenu* (cow of plenty). Immortality is the milk that it yields. The feet of the Lord constitute its place of residence.

69

जडता पशुता कलङ्किता
कुटिलचरत्वं च नास्ति मयि देव ।
अस्ति यदि राजमौले
भवदाभरणस्य नास्मि किं पात्रम् ॥

jaḍatā paśutā kalaṅkitā
kuṭilacaratvam ca nāsti mayi deva|
asti yadi rājamaule
bhavad-ābharaṇasya nāsmi kiṁ pātram||

Inertness, animality, impuriy, and crookedness of movement are not in me, O God! Even if they be, O Crescent-crested One, am I not fit to serve as Thy ornament ?

The devotee tells the Lord that he is fit to be accepted by Him. The very fact that he is a devotee shows that there are no blemishes in him. He has intelligence, humanity, purity, and straight-forwardness as the governing virtues. Even supposing that the devotee does not possess these virtues, but only the opposite vices, Śiva has no right to reject him. For, has He not accepted as adornments inert, non-human, impure and crooked objects, such as hides, deer, bull, crescent-moon, and serpents?

Or, all these defects may be regarded as belonging to the crescent-moon. Śiva is pleased to wear the extremely defective moon as His head-ornament. Why, then, should not the devotee claim to be accepted by Him ? The devotee's character, certainly, does not have so many blemishes as the moon's.

Candra (moon) is in the masculine gender. There are different versions of the circumstance which led to Śiva's acceptance of Candra as head-ornament. One of them is as follows: Dakṣa, one of the first agents of creation (*Prajāpati*), gave his twenty-seven daughters (stars) in marriage to Candra, on condition that Candra should treat them all alike, without showing favouritism to any. But Candra developed a special attachment to Rohiṇī. The other sisters got piqued, and complained to their father. Dakṣa flew into a rage and cursed Candra saying that he would get wasted, that he would lose one of his *kalās* each day, and that when all the sixteen *kalās* vanished he would fade away. On the sixteenth day, there was only one *kalā* left. Candra took refuge in the Lord. The Lord accepted him and placed him on his head as an ornament. By His grace, Candra began to regain his lost *kalās* at the rate of one each day. The Lord willed that Dakṣa's curse also should not go in vain. Therefore, he decreed that the waxing and the waning of the moon should alternate.

According to another story, a curse fell upon Candra because he had sought to defile the bed of his teacher's wife.

70

अरहसि रहसि स्वतंत्रबुद्ध्या
वरिवसितुं सुलभः प्रसन्नमूर्तिः ।
अगणितफलदायकः प्रभुर्मे
जगदधिको हृदि राजशेखरोऽस्ति ॥

arahasi rahasi svatantra-buddhyā
varivasituṁ sulabhaḥ prasannamūrtiḥ|
agaṇitaphaladāyakaḥ prabhur me
jagadadhiko hṛdi rājaśekharo'sti||

In the open and in secret, He is easy to live with, with a mind that is independent; He has a form that is gracious; He is the giver of measureless fruit, the Lord who exceeds the world: the Crescent-crested One who resides in the Heart !

God is transcendent as well as immanent. He exceeds the world (*jagadadhikaḥ*), and yet resides in the heart (*hṛdi asti*). To live with Him ought to be the easiest thing. But it seems to be very difficult for those who have not begun to feel His grace. He is graciousness itself; and He is the giver of *mokṣa*.

arahasi, 'in the world without'; *rahasi*, 'in the heart within'.
For *jagadadhikaḥ*, an alternative reading is: *jagadadhipaḥ*, meaning 'the Lord of the world'.

71

आरूढभक्तिगुणकुञ्चितभावचाप-
युक्तैः शिवस्मरणबाणगणैरमोघैः ।
निर्जित्य किल्बिषरिपून्विजयी सुधीन्द्रः
सानन्दमावहति सुस्थिरराजलक्ष्मीम् ॥

ārūḍhabhakti-guṇakuñcita-bhāvacāpa-
yuktaiḥ śiva-smaraṇa-bāṇagaṇair amoghaiḥ|
nirjitya kilbiṣaripūn vijayī sudhīndraḥ
sānandam āvahati susthirarājalakṣmīm||

With the unerring arrows of Śiva-remembrance fixed to the bow of meditation bent with the string of firm devotion, the one who has a good mind conquers the enemies that are sins, and gains the royal wealth of stability endowed with bliss.

The devotee is, here, compared to an expert archer. A royal prince who wishes to gain a kingdom should destroy his enemies in a straight fight; in order to accomplish this, he must have a strong arm and skill in fighting. In the spiritual fight with evil, the bow to be used is meditation, and the arrow, remembrance of Śiva. The devotee wields this weapon in a sure and expert manner, overcomes ignorance and its brood, and gains the supreme goal, *mokṣa*.

72

ध्यानाञ्जनेन समवेक्ष्य तमःप्रदेशं
भित्त्वा महाबलिभिरीश्वरनाममन्त्रैः ।
दिव्याश्रितं भुजगभूषणमुद्वहन्ति
ये पादपद्ममिह ते शिव ते कृतार्थाः ॥

dhyānāñjanena samavekṣya tamaḥpradeśaṁ
bhittvā mahābalibhir īśvaranāma-mantraiḥ|
divyāśritaṁ bhujagabhūṣaṇam udvahanti
ye pādapadmam iha te śiva te kṛtārthāḥ||

O Śiva? They indeed, are those who have gained their end, — they who, here, have reached Thy lotus-feet which are the refuge of the gods and which wear serpents as ornaments, after acquiring a clear vision through the ointment of meditation and after breaking through the region of darkness through making ritual offerings consisting in the name-formulas of the Lord.

The one who wants to come by a buried treasure applies first some kind of magical ointment to his eyes so that he may have a vision of the treasure. Then, he digs up the earth at the right place, offers oblations to the deity guarding treasures, and thus gains his end.

Here, the riches to be gained are the Lord's feet; the ointment is meditation; the hard crust to be removed is ignorance; and the oblations are the uttering of the names of Śiva.

73

भूदारतामुदवहद्यदपेक्षया श्री-
भूदार एव किमतः सुमते लभस्व ।
केदारमाकलितमुक्तिमहौषधीनां
पादारविन्दभजनं परमेश्वरस्य ॥

bhūdāratām udavahad yadapekṣayā śrī-
bhūdāra eva kimataḥ sumate labhasva|
kedāram ākalita-mukti-mahauṣadhīnāṁ
pādāravinda-bhajanaṁ parameśvarasya||

O Good Mind! Do get to adore the lotus-feet of the supreme Lord which are the field for the growth of the medicinal herb of release that is desired by all—the feet for gaining which even Viṣṇu, the lord of Śrī and Bhū, took the form of a boar. What else should one do ?

Here, again, is the analogy of agriculture. The Lord's feet are the fertile fields on which the cure-herb of *mokṣa* grows.

In praising the Lord's feet, the story of Viṣṇu making a futile attempt to reach them is, again, alluded to.

74

आशापाशक्लेशदुर्वासनादि-
भेदोद्युक्तैर्दिव्यगन्धैरमन्दैः ।
आशाशाटीकस्य पादारविन्दं
चेतःपेटीं वासितां मे तनोतु ॥

āśāpāśakleśa-durvāsanādi-
bhedodyuktair divyagandhair amandaiḥ|
āśāśāṭikasya pādāravindaṁ
cetaḥpeṭīṁ vāsitāṁ me tanotu||

May the lotus-feet of the Lord whose virtues are the cardinal directions of space make the box of my heart sweet-smelling through the strong divine scents that overpower the bad odours of desire, delusion, passion, etc.

The mind is, here, compared to a closed box, filled with bad odours—delusion, desires, passions, etc. And, the Lord is requested to open it and make it smell sweet.

75

कल्याणिनं सरसचित्रगतिं सवेगं
सर्वेङ्गितज्ञमनघं ध्रुवलक्षणाढ्यम् ।
चेतस्तुरङ्गमधिरुह्य चर स्मरारे
नेतः समस्तजगतां वृषभाधिरूढ ॥

kalyāṇinaṁ sarasacitragatiṁ savegaṁ
sarveṅgitajñam anaghaṁ dhruvalakṣaṇāḍhyam|
cetasturaṅgam adhiruhya cara smarāre
netaḥ samasta-jagatāṁ vṛṣabhādhirūḍha||

O Destroyer of Passion! O Leader of all the worlds! O Rider of the Bull! Move about, mounting my mind-horse which is auspicious, which can move quickly and in various ways, which has speed, which can understand all signs, which is without blemish, and which is endowed with stable characteristics.

Śiva is the overlord of all the worlds. He is our great leader in the fight against passion. The Purāṇas tell us that the God of lust, Manmatha, was burnt by Him. Śiva has to go wherever He is called—and that, quickly—in order to save plaintive souls. How can He do this if He only uses the Bull as His vehicle? Such a slow-moving mount is no good. The devotee places at the Lord's service a good, fast-moving horse, his mind. Let the Lord ride this horse, harnessing it to do His bidding.

The story of the burning of Manmatha (also called Kāma, Smara) is this: Dakṣa performed a sacrifice to which he did not invite Śiva, his son-in-law. Dākṣāyaṇī, Śiva's consort, went to her father's place only to get insulted. She committed suicide by falling into the sacrificial fire. Śiva, on coming to know of this, caused the sacrifice to be destroyed. Dākṣāyaṇī was reborn as Pārvatī, daughter of Himavān (Himālayas). With a view to regain her Lord, she performed austerities. But Śiva was lost in meditation, unconcerned with the world. Harrassed by the demon Tāraka, the gods wished that a son should be born to Śiva and Pārvatī, who alone could kill Tāraka. They sent Manmatha, the god of love, to rouse in Śiva's heart an interest in Pārvatī. When Manmatha was trying his best to draw Śiva out of His meditation, Śiva opened His third eye, the eye in the forehead, and burned Manmatha. Hence, Śiva is called Kāmāri, Smarāri.

76

भक्तिर्महेशपदपुष्करमावसन्ती
कादम्बिनीव कुरुते परितोषवर्षम् ।
संपूरितो भवति यस्य मनस्तटाक-
स्तज्जन्मसस्यमखिलं सफलं च नान्यत् ॥

bhaktir maheśapada-puṣkaram āvasantī
kādambinīva kurute paritoṣavarṣam|
sampūrito bhavati yasya manastaṭākas-
tajjanma-sasyam akhilaṁ saphalaṁ ca nānyat||

Devotion, like the cloud, residing in the sky which is the great Lord, sends forth the shower of bliss: he, the lake of whose mind gets filled, reaps the entire crop of life; not any other.

Here once again, is the analogy of agriculture. It is the mind that is filled with devotion to God that will gain the final goal, *mokṣa*.

77

बुद्धिः स्थिरा भवितुमीश्वरपादपद्म-
सक्ता वधूर्विरहिणीव सदा स्मरन्ती ।
सद्भावनास्मरणदर्शनकीर्तनादि
संमोहितेव शिवमन्त्रजपेन विन्ते ॥

buddhiḥ sthirā bhavitum īśvarapādapadma-
saktā vadhūr virahiṇīva sadā smarantī|
sadbhāvanā-smaraṇa-darśana-kīrtanādi
saṁmohiteva śivamantrajapena vinte||

O Lord! Like a woman separated from her husband, the mind that is attached to the lotus-feet constantly remembers in order to become firm, and being charmed by the muttering of *Śivamantra*, it engages itself in good thoughts, memory, sight, singing, etc.

The devotee's mind is compared to a woman separated from her husband. The mind cannot bear the separation from the Lord. No other thoughts have any room in it. It constantly thinks of Him. And, the Lord becomes the only concern of the various faculties such as seeing, speaking, remembering, etc.

78

सदुपचारविधिष्वनुबोधितां
सविनयां सुहृदं समुपाश्रिताम् ।
मम समुद्धर बुद्धिमिमां प्रभो
वरगुणेन नवोढवधूमिव ॥

sadupacāravidhiṣv-anubodhitāṁ
savinayāṁ suhṛdaṁ samupāśritām|
mama samuddhara buddhim imāṁ prabho
varaguṇena navoḍhavadhūm iva||

O Lord! Do uplift this intellect of mine, as one would a new bride, by endowing it with supreme excellence—the intellect which is instructed in the ways of good service, which is humble, which is good-hearted, and which has the good as its resort.

The language of bridal mysticism employed in the previous verse is continued here. The intellect is the bride endowed with all the virtues. She has all the qualifications required to become the bride of God. Let Him come and wed this bride.

79

नित्यं योगिमनःसरोजदलसंचारक्षमस्त्वत्क्रमः
शम्भो तेन कथं कठोरयमराड्वक्षःकवाटक्षतिः ।
अत्यन्तं मृदुलं त्वदङ्घ्रियुगलं हा मे मनश्चिन्तय-
त्येतल्लोचनगोचरं कुरु विभो हस्तेन संवाहये ॥

nityaṁ yogimanaḥ-saroja-dala-saṁcāra-kṣamas tvatkramaḥ
śambho tena kathaṁ kaṭhora-yamarāḍ-vakṣaḥkavāṭa-kṣatiḥ|

atyantaṁ mṛdulaṁ tvadaṅghriyugalaṁ hā me manaś cintayaty-
etal-locanagocaraṁ kuru vibho hastena saṁvāhaye||

O Śaṁbhu! Thy feet are ever accustomed to walk on the lotus-petals of the yogins' minds. How, then, could they kick at the hard chest-door of Yama? Very tender are Thy feet! Ah, my mind ponders! O Lord! Bring them within the sphere of my sight; I shall bear them with my hands.

In verse 64, reference was made to the hard tasks that the tender feet of Śiva have to perform. Among them is the kicking at the chest of Yama. In the present verse, Yama's chest is compared to a strong door. By contrast, the minds of Yogins are like lotus petals. The Lord's feet are used to walking on these petals; and this is only proper. But how can His feet bear the rough usage as against Yama's chest? The devotee longs to massage the holy feet, and implores the Lord to reveal them.

80

एष्यत्येष जनिं मनोऽस्य कठिनं तस्मिन्नटानीति म-
द्रक्षायै गिरिसीम्नि कोमलपदन्यासः पुराभ्यासितः ।
नो चेद्दिव्यगृहान्तरेषु सुमनस्तल्पेषु वेद्यादिषु
प्रायः सत्सु शिलातलेषु नटनं शंभो किमर्थं तव ॥

eṣyaty-eṣa janiṁ mano'sya kaṭhinaṁ tasmin-naṭānīti mad-
rakṣāyai girisīmni komalapadanyāsaḥ purābhyāsitaḥ|
no ced-divyagṛhāntareṣu sumanastalpeṣu vedyādiṣu
prāyaḥ satsu śilātaleṣu naṭanaṁ śaṁbho kimarthaṁ tava||

"This one is going to be born. His mind is hard. I have to dance on it." Thinking thus in order to protect me, Thou didst practise placing Thy tender steps, in former times, on Mountain ridges, O Śaṁbhu! Otherwise, while there are the insides of divine houses, flowery bedsteads, covered verandahs, etc., in abundance, why didst Thou dance in rocky regions?

In the previous verse, the devotee wondered how the Lord's tender feet could bear the strain of kicking at Yama's hard chest. In the present verse, the devotee remembers that his own mind is made of very hard stuff. The Lord may not enter it saying that it is too hard for His tender feet. But, says the devotee, such an excuse is not available to the Lord. The Lord had known that the soul was going to be born, that its mind would be hard, and that He would have to use it as His dance-ground. It was because of this fore-knowledge that He chose the Mountain as His habitation, so that His feet might get used to walking on hard ground. What other reason could there be for this choice? It was not as if there was no better place for the Lord to reside in. There are plenty of them—the hearts of gods, the minds of good and pious people, the altars where ritual offerings are made, etc.

81

कंचित्कालमुमामहेश भवत. पादारविन्दार्चनैः
कंचिद्ध्यानसमाधिभिश्च नतिभिः कंचित्कथाकर्णनैः
कंचित्कंचिदवेक्षणैश्च नुतिभिः कंचिद्दशामीदृशीं
यः प्राप्नोति मुदा त्वदर्पितमना जीवन्स मुक्तः खलु ॥

kaṁcit-kālam umāmaheśa bhavataḥ pādāravindārcanaiḥ
kaṁcid-dhyānasamādhibhiś ca natibhiḥ kaṁcit-kathākarṇanaiḥ|
kaṁcit-kaṁcid-avekṣaṇaiś ca nutibhiḥ kaṁcid daśām īdṛśīṁ
yaḥ prāpnoti mudā tvadarpitamanā jīvan sa muktaḥ khalu||

O Consort of Umā! Sometime in worshipping Thy lotus-feet, sometime in meditation and concentration, sometime in offering obeisance, sometime in listening to (Thy) stories, sometime in looking at (Thy) form, sometime in singing (Thy) praise—he who gains such a state in exultation, having surrendered his mind to Thee, is verily a *jīvan-mukta* !

Devotion, when it becomes mature, leads to *jīvanmukti*, liberation-in-life. The fruit of devotion is not an unseen result; it is to be enjoyed here and now. When the mind has been surrendered to God, the mind ceases to be. This is the state of mindlessness (*amanībhāva*). It is the mind that binds the soul; it is the mind that liberates. The mind that is attached to external objects binds; the mind that is attached to God liberates.

82

बाणत्वं वृषभत्वमर्धवपुषा भार्यात्वमार्यापते
घोणित्वं सखिता मृदङ्गवहता चेत्यादि रूपं दधौ ।
त्वत्पादे नयनार्पणं च कृतवांस्त्वद्देहभागो हरिः
पूज्यात्पूज्यतरः स एव हि न चेत्को वा तदन्योऽधिकः ॥

bāṇatvaṁ vṛṣabhatvam ardhavapuṣā bhāryātvam āryāpate
ghoṇitvaṁ sakhitā mṛdaṅgavahatā cetyādi rūpaṁ dadhau|
tvat-pāde nayanārpaṇaṁ ca kṛtavāṁs tvad-dehabhāgo hariḥ
pūjyāt-pūjyataraḥ sa eva hi na cet ko vā tadanyo'dhikaḥ||

O Consort of Devi! Hari, indeed, took many forms— that of an arrow, that of a bull, that of a wife occupying half the body, that of a boar, that of a friend, that bearing a drum, etc.; he also offered his eye at Thy feet. That one, who forms part of Thy body, is verily the most worshipful; for who can excel him?

Here, the Hari-Hara form is celebrated. Viṣṇu (Hari) is associated with Śiva (Hara) in several ways. (1) He became the arrow with which Śiva destroyed the three cities. (2) He serves as the vehicle, Bull, for Śiva. (3). He became the wife of Śiva, occupying half His body. (4) He took the form of a boar in order to reach Śiva's feet by burrowing the earth. (5) He served as Śiva's companion, taking the form of a ravishingly beautiful maiden (*Mohinī*), (a) for distributing ambrosia to the gods and for seeing that the demons did not get it, and (b) for destroying Bhasmāsura who had gained from Śiva the power of burning all those on whose heads he chose to place his hand. (6) Viṣṇu beats the drum as Śiva dances. (7) When He found, while performing *arcana* to Śiva, that He was short of one thousand lotuses by one, He offered His eye in the place of the lotus.

Hari is the nearest to Hara, and is greater than all other gods.

83

जननमृतियुतानां सेवया देवतानां
न भवति सुखलेशः संशयो नास्ति तत्र ।
अजनिममृतरूपं साम्बमीशं भजन्ते
य इह परमसौख्यं ते हि धन्या लभन्ते ॥

jananamṛtiyutānāṁ sevayā devatānāṁ
na bhavati sukhaleśaḥ saṁśayo nāsti tatra|
ajanim amṛtarūpaṁ sāṁbam īśaṁ bhajante
ya iha paramasaukhyaṁ te hi dhanyā labhante||

There results not even the least trace of happiness from worshipping the gods that are endowed with birth and death; in regard to this, there is no doubt. They who adore, here, the Lord of Pārvatī who has no birth and is eternal, are, indeed fortunate; they gain the supreme happiness.

An idea with which we are familiar is repeated here. There is no use of worshipping the minor gods and godlings. They cannot help us in gaining the final goal, perfection. Śiva alone, who is eternal, can save the soul by granting it supreme happiness.

84

शिव तव परिचर्यासंनिधानाय गौर्या
भव मम गुणधुर्यां बुद्धिकन्यां प्रदास्ये ।
सकलभुवनबन्धो सच्चिदानन्दसिन्धो
सदय हृदयगेहे सर्वदा संवस त्वम् ॥

śiva tava paricaryā sāṁnidhānāya gauryā
bhava mama guṇadhuryāṁ buddhikanyāṁ pradāsye|
sakalabhuvanabandho saccidānandasindho
sadaya hṛdayagehe sarvadā saṁvasa tvam||

O Śiva! O Bhava! O Friend of all the worlds! O Ocean of Existence-Consciousness-Bliss! O compassionate One! To be with Gaurī engaged in Thy service, I give my mind-maiden who is endowed with excellences. Do Thou dwell always in the house of my heart!

The devotee dedicates his daughter, Mind, to the service of the Lord. Let Mind be with Pārvatī and serve the Lord along with Her! Let the Lord deign to use the Heart as His place of residence! Let Him always live there, and never leave it!

85

जलधिमथनदक्षो नैव पातालभेदी
न च वनमृगयायां नैव लुब्धः प्रवीणः।
अशनकुसुमभूषावस्त्रमुख्यां सपर्यां
कथय कथमहं ते कल्पयानीन्दुमौले ॥

jaladhimathanadakṣo naiva pātālabhedī
na ca vanamṛgayāyāṁ naiva lubdhaḥ pravīṇaḥ|
aśanakusumabhūṣāvastramukhyāṁ saparyāṁ
kathaya katham ahaṁ te kalpayānīndumaule||

O Crescent-crested Lord! I am not skilled in churning the ocean; nor in splitting the nether-world; nor am I a hunter, expert in hunting game. How, then, may I offer Thee, in worship (materials such as) food (poison), flower (serpents), ornament (serpents), clothing (the hide of the elephant), etc.? Do tell me!

The devotee is at a loss to know how he is to worship the Lord. The things that are acceptable to the Lord, he is incapable of procuring. Poison is Śiva's food. Unless the milk-ocean is churned, Śiva's food cannot be procured. Serpents form Śiva's adornments. In order to procure them, one should go to the nether-world. Śiva's clothing consists of the hide of elephant and tiger's skin. For getting these, one must be an expert hunter. The devotee says, "As I do not possess any of these abilities, how am I to offer anything to Thee?"

86

पूजाद्रव्यसमृद्धयो विरचिताः पूजां कथं कुर्महे
पक्षित्वं न च वा किटित्वमपि न प्राप्तं मया दुर्लभम ।
जाने मस्तकमङ्घ्रिपल्लवमुमाजाने न तेऽहं विभो
न ज्ञातं हि पितामहेन हरिणा तत्वेन तद्रूपिणा ॥

pūjādravyasamṛddhayo viracitāḥ pūjāṁ kathaṁ kurmahe
pakṣītvaṁ na ca vā kiṭitvaṁ api na prāptaṁ mayā durlabham|
jāne mastakam aṅghripallavam umājāne na te'haṁ vibho
na jñātaṁ hi pitāmahena hariṇā tattvena tadrūpiṇā||

O Consort of Pārvatī! The materials for worship have been gathered. But how shall I perform the worship? I have not gained the status of a bird or that of a boar,—which is difficult of attainment. O all-pervading One! I do not see Thy crown or Thy lotus-feet. Verily they were not seen even by Brahmā and Viṣṇu who had assumed those forms!

Granting that one has somehow gathered all the materials required for the worship of Śiva how is one to perform the worship? It is not possible to see either the head or the feet of Śiva. Even Brahmā and Viṣṇu could not see them. How, then, is worship to be offered?

87

अशनं गरलं फणी कलापो
वसनं चर्म च वाहनं महोक्षः ।

मम दास्यसि किं किमस्ति शंभो
तव पादाम्बुजभक्तिमेव देहि ॥

aśanaṁ garalaṁ phaṇī kalāpo
vasanaṁ carma ca vāhanaṁ mahokṣaḥ|
mama dāsyasi kiṁ kimasti śaṁbho
tava pādāmbuja-bhaktim eva dehi||

O Śaṁbhu! Thy food is poison, ornament serpent, clothing hide, and transport the great bull. What wilt Thou give me? And, what (else) is there? Grant me only devotion unto Thy lotus-feet.

In verse 85, the devotee said, "How can I offer Thee the things that are meet for Thee—things such as poison, serpents, and hides?" In the present verse, he says, "What useful thing is there that Thou canst give me? The things that are with Thee, such as poison, etc., are not useful to me. I ask only for devotion unto Thy feet".

This verse is a *nindāstuti*, praise disguised as blame.

88

यदा कृताम्भोनिधिसेतुबन्धनः
करस्थलाधःकृतपर्वताधिपः ।
भवानि ते लङ्घितपद्मसंभव-
स्तदा शिवार्चास्तवभावनक्षमः ॥

yadā kṛtāmbhonidhisetubandhanaḥ
karasthalādhaḥkṛtaparvatādhipaḥ|
bhavāni te laṅghitapadmasaṁbhavas
tadā śivārcāstavabhāvanakṣamaḥ||

O Śiva! It is only when I become the one who built a bridge on the ocean (Rāma), or the one who pressed down the Vindhya mountain with the palm of his hand (Agastya), or surpass the lotus-born Brahmā (who creates the worlds and reveals the Vedas) that I shall be able to worship Thee, sing Thy praise, and meditate on Thee.

It is not possible for an ordinary mortal to worship Śiva, utter His praise, or meditate on him. In order to be able to do these, one should be either a Rāmacandra, or an Agastya, or a Brahmā. Śrī Rāmacandra, who built the bridge to Laṅkā, offered worship to the Lord at Rāmeśvaram. Agastya, the sage-dwarf, quelled the pride of Mount Vindhya by pressing it down with the palm of his hand; he could sing the Lord's praise. One would have to excel the creator Brahmā, if one were to meditate on Śiva.

89

नतिभिर्नुतिभिस्त्वमीश पूजा-
विधिभिर्ध्यानसमाधिभिर्न तुष्टः ।
धनुषा मुसलेन चाश्मभिर्वा
वद ते प्रीतिकरं तथा करोमि ॥

natibhir-nutibhis tvam īśa pūjā-
vidhibhir-dhyānasamādhibhir na tuṣṭaḥ|
dhanuṣā musalena cāśmabhirvā
vada te prītikaraṁ tathā karomi||

O Lord! Thou art not pleased with offerings of obeisance, singings of praise, procedures of worship, meditations and concentrations. If through (hitting with) a bow, a pylon or stones (Thou art pleased), tell me so; I shall do what pleases Thee.

The present verse, again, is in the form of *nindāstuti*. The conventional modes of worship do not seem to please Śiva. Otherwise, why did He accept strange and rude forms of adoration ?

(1) Arjuna performed austerities in order to gain the grace of Śiva. Śiva appeared before him disguised as a hunter. A quarrel ensued between the two over an animal which he

claimed he had shot. This led to a scuffle, and Arjuna beat the Lord with his bow. This pleased the Lord greatly.

(2) Śīlavatī was a lady who was employed by people who wanted their paddy milled. The payment she received from them was in the form of rice which she would cook and offer first to the devotees of Lord Śiva before taking it herself. She regarded her simple work as a *sādhana* and philosophical teachings would come to her in that way. She became well known for her devotion and wisdom and thus she was greatly respected by all. Her only son was equal to her in devotion and piety. While engaged in grazing cattle Śīlavatī's cow-herd son spent his time in philosophic truth-inquiry. He too was revered by the villagers as was his mother.

On a *pradoṣa* evening, while Śiva was beginning His cosmic dance, Śiruttoṇḍar, a devotee, who to mark his devotion to the Lord, sacrificed his son, became highly indignant at being pushed aside by Nandikeśvara (the divine bull-attendant of Lord Śiva). Noticing the devotee's pride the Lord invited Śiruttoṇḍar to join Him in descending to Śīlavatī's humble abode.

Disguised as *Śiva-bhaktas* they entered Śīlavatī's house asking for food although they knew that she had just finished feeding the devotees. To gain time the pious lady requested the two holy ones to finish their ablutions while she could prepare the food for them. On the way to the tank the ascetics met with Śīlavatī's son. They told him that he was requested to come home and have his meal and that they would follow shortly. The pious son refused owing to his responsibility of caring for the cattle. On being persuaded that the elder ascetic would himself look after the cows, the young man returned to his house and finding the food ready, served himself. As he was about to finish, his mother came inside still holding the pylon in her hand, having just discharged her debt caused by the unexpected arrival of the two ascetics. She could hear one of them singing a song. It was on the futility of relationships with family members and in praise of feeding devotees of God. She flew at her son who had unknowingly committed this terrible mistake. The horrified boy tried to explain that the Lord's concern is certainly for *Śiva-bhaktas* but also for all other living beings and that thus He would not regard the mistake committed as a sin. But Śīlavatī's anger was not appeased. She furiously struck the boy with her pylon. Then she hid her son's dead body in the kitchen and went to invite the guests for their meal. In the meantime the cows had come back to the village alone before the usual time. The astonished villagers called out to her inquiring as to the whereabouts of her cow-herd son. Hearing all this the elder ascetic exclaimed that it would not be possible to take food excluding such a lovable boy. Realising the whole truth by now, Śīlavatī, in her determination to feed the Lord as she saw fit, she threatened even Him with her pylon, forbidding Him to leave the house. Having taken the food the Lord simply disappeared, leaving Śīlavatī frantic with grief. She implored Him not to forsake her who was of a low caste since He is known to have showered His grace on even coarse devotion by sincere devotees who were ignorant of the proper manners of worship. In the meantime the son came back to life and ran to her embracing her warmly. After examining him in amazement Śīlavatī told him what had taken place. The boy consoled his mother and resolved to sing in praise of God-head. Lord Viṣṇu appeared followed by the other Deities. Both Śīlavatī and her son prayed for release from the cycle of birth and death. The Gods were greatly pleased by the total devotion of Śīlavatī and while they were bestowing their grace Śiruttoṇḍar, ashamed and humbled, bowed his head before her. Lord Śiva told the son that he could ask for a boon. The boy requested Him to bless him with permanent *darśan* as also that He take residence in his heart. The Lord sent both mother and son to Kailāsa in the *Indra-Vimānam*. Celestial music was heard by all the people who were present as witnesses of this divine spectacle. The Lord disappeared with His entourage after establishing the teaching that irrespective of caste or creed, all sincere and ardent devotees of God, if they surrender their all to Him, will reach their goal.

Probably Śaṅkara refers to this story when he says about worship offered by threatening to beat with a pylon.

(3) Śākya Nāyanār, who lived under the regime of Śamaṇas, could not worship the Lord in the conventional manner with flowers. He pelted stones, intsead, at the Lord's image, and offered heartworship.

90

वचसा चरितं वदामि शंभो-
रहमुद्योगविधासु तेऽप्रसक्तः ।
मनसाकृतिमीश्वरस्य सेवे
शिरसा चैव सदाशिवं नमामि ॥

vacasā caritaṁ vadāmi śaṁbhor-
aham udyogavidhāsu te'prasaktaḥ|
manasākṛtim īśvarasya seve
śirasā caiva sadāśivaṁ namāmi||

I am unused to the methods of meditating on Thee with effort. I shall utter through speech the story of Śaṁbhu; shall adore with the mind the form of the Lord; and shall bow with the head to Sadāśiva.

If one has not yet gained the competence to offer heart-worship to the Lord, let him not lose heart. Let him begin with the lower modes of devotion; and he will be eventually lifted to the higher levels.

91

आद्याविद्या हृद्गता निर्गतासी-
द्विद्या हृद्या हृद्गता त्वत्प्रसादात् ।
सेवे नित्यं श्रीकरं त्वत्पदाब्जं
भावे मुक्तेर्भाजनं राजमौले ॥

ādyāvidyā hṛdgatā nirgatāsīd-
vidyā hṛdyā hṛdgatā tvat-prasādāt|
seve nityaṁ śrīkaraṁ tvat-padābjaṁ
bhāve mukter bhājanaṁ rājamaule||

O Crescent-crested Lord! Through Thy grace the beginningless nescience resident in the heart has been removed; and the delectable (Brahman-) knowledge has taken its seat in the heart. Thy lotus-feet, which bring auspiciousness and are the repositories of liberation, I meditate on and adore.

The supreme end of devotion to Śiva is *mokṣa*, liberation from bondage. Nescience is the cause of bondage. Wisdom is what removes nescience. It is God's grace that grants wisdom.

92

दूरीकृतानि दुरितानि दुरक्षराणि
दौर्भाग्यदुःखदुरहंकृतिदुर्वचांसि ।
सारं त्वदीयचरितं नितरां पिबन्तं
गौरीश मामिह समुद्धर सत्कटाक्षैः ॥

dūrīkṛtāni duritāni durakṣarāṇi
daurbhāgya-duḥkha-durahaṁkṛtidurvacāṁsi|
sāraṁ tvadīyacaritaṁ nitarāṁ pibantaṁ
gaurīśa māṁ iha samuddhara satkaṭākṣaiḥ||

O Consort of Gaurī! Ill-fortune, misery, bad egoity, and wicked speech, which are the result of the bad fates and sins, have been driven away. Me, who am drinking deeply the sweet story of Thy greatness, please do save, here.

It is through God's grace that every thing that is bad is removed. Evil, sin, misery—all these disappear like mist before the rising sun of divine grace.

93

सोमकलाधरमौलौ
कोमलघनकंधरे महामहसि ।
स्वामिनि गिरिजानाथे
मामकहृदयं निरन्तर रमताम् ॥

somakalādharamaulau
komalaghanakaṁdhare mahāmahasi|
svāmini girijānāthe
māmakahṛdayaṁ nirantaraṁ ramatām||

Let my heart ever revel in the Lord who is the Consort of Girijā, who wears on his crest the Crescent-moon, whose throat is beautifully blue like the cloud, and who has a greatly luminous form.

The devotee recapitulates some of the deeds of grace performed by the Lord and meditates on their deep significance. The very form and features of the Lord remind one of these deeds.

94

सा रसना ते नयने
तावेव करौ स एव कृतकृत्यः ।
या ये यौ यो भर्गं
वदतीक्षेते सदार्चतः स्मरति ॥

sā rasanā te nayane
tāveva karau sa eva kṛtakṛtyaḥ|
yā ye yau yo bhargaṁ
vadatīkṣete sadārcataḥ smarati||

That is tongue which speaks of the glorious Śiva; those are eyes which behold (Him); those are hands which always worship (Him); he alone is the one who has gained his end, who (ever) remembers (Him).

An idea expressed in several verses earlier is repeated here. The functions of the sense-organs and the mind should all be directed towards the Lord.

95

अतिमृदुलौ मम चरणा-
वतिकठिनं ते मनो भवानीश ।
इति विचिकित्सां संत्यज
शिव कथमासीद् गिरौ तथा प्रवेशः ॥

atimṛdulau mama caraṇāv-
atikaṭhinaṁ te mano bhavānīśa|
iti vicikitsāṁ saṁtyaja
śiva katham āsid girau tathā praveśaḥ||

O Consort of Pārvatī! Do relinquish the idea, "My feet are too tender; your mind is too hard". O Śiva! How, then, didst Thou come to have Thy residence on the mountains?

Here, again, is repeated a request to the Lord already expressed by the devotee. The Lord should not refuse to enter the mind saying that it is too hard for His tender feet.

96

धैर्याङ्कुशेन निभृतं रभसादाकृष्य भक्तिशृङ्खलया ।
पुरहर चरणालाने हृदयमदेभं बधान चिद्यन्त्रैः ॥

dhairyāṅkuśena nibhṛtaṁ
rabhasād ākṛṣya bhaktiśṛṅkhalayā|
purahara caraṇālāne
hṛdayamadebhaṁ badhāna cidyantraiḥ||

O Destroyer of the Cities! Do bind the elephant of my heart to the peg of Thy feet with the chain of devotion, dragging it speedily with the help of the goad of courage and the machinery of intelligence, so that it may not stray.

In this verse and the next, the mind is compared to an elephant. This wild elephant should be captured and brought under check. The Lord alone can do it.

97

प्रचरत्यभितः प्रगल्भवृत्त्या
मदवानेष मनःकरी गरीयान् ।
परिगृह्य नयेन भक्तिरज्ज्वा
परम स्थाणुपदं दृढं नयामुम् ॥

pracaraty-abhitaḥ pragalbhavṛttyā
madavān eṣa manaḥkarī garīyān|
parigṛhya nayena bhaktirajjvā
parama sthāṇupadaṁ dṛḍhaṁ nayāmum||

O Supreme Lord! This mind-elephant is in rut and is mighty; doing daring deeds, it roams about in all directions; with the cord of devotion seize it tactfully and lead it firmly to the place of stability.

The mind-elephant, which misbehaves and is wayward, should be controlled by being bound with the cord of devotion; and slowly it should be led to the feet of the Lord, its stables, and made to rest there. *Sthāṇu*, the Stable, is an appellation of Śiva.

98

सर्वालङ्कारयुक्तां सरलपदयुतां साधुवृत्तां सुवर्णां
सद्भिः संस्तूयमानां सरसगुणयुतां लक्षितां लक्षणाढ्याम् ।
उद्यद्भूषाविशेषामुपगतविनयां द्योतमानार्थरेखां
कल्याणीं देव गौरीप्रिय मम कविताकन्यकां त्वं गृहाण ॥

sarvālaṅkārayuktāṁ saralapadayutāṁ sādhuvṛttāṁ suvarṇāṁ
sadbhiḥ saṁstūyamānāṁ sarasaguṇayutāṁ lakṣitāṁ lakṣaṇāḍhyām|
udyadbhūṣāviśeṣām upagatavinayāṁ dyotamānārtharekhāṁ
kalyāṇīṁ deva gaurīpriya mama kavitākanyakāṁ tvaṁ gṛhāṇa||

O Beloved of Gaurī! O God! Do accept my daughter, Poesy, who has all the embellishments, who has a graceful gait, who is given to the ways of piety, who is fair, who is praised by the good, who has pleasing manners, who is an ideal (bride), who is endowed with good characteristics, who wears shining ornaments, who is modest, who bears clear marks of fortune (on her palm), and who is auspicious.

The poet makes an offering of his poem to the Lord, as a parent would offer his daughter in marriage to the groom he has chosen. As applied to the poem, the characteristics would be the following: the poem has all the *alaṅkāras*; its words are graceful; fine metres have been employed in its composition; it is beautiful; it deserves the praise of all good people; it teems with the various good *rasas*; its aim is good; its features are good: it has all the excellences; it is expressive of humility; it shines with deep and suggestive meanings; it confers auspiciousness on its readers.

99

इदं ते युक्तं वा परमशिव कारुण्यजलधे
गतौ तिर्यग्रूपं तव पदशिरोदर्शनधिया ।
हरिब्रह्माणौ तौ दिवि भुवि चरन्तौ श्रमयुतौ
कथं शंभो स्वामिन्कथय मम वेद्योऽसि पुरतः ॥

idaṁ te yuktaṁ vā paramaśiva kāruṇyajaladhe
gatau tiryagrūpaṁ tava padaśirodarśanadhiyā|
haribrahmāṇau tau divi bhuvi carantau śramayutau
kathaṁ śaṁbho svāmin kathaya mama vedyo'si purataḥ||

O Supreme Śiva! O Ocean of Compassion! With a view to behold Thy feet and head, Viṣṇu and Brahmā took sub-human forms; moving about beneath the earth and in the sky, they suffered. Is this proper for Thee? O Śaṁbhu! O Master! Tell me how Thou wilt become revealed to me immediately.

The story of the failure of Brahmā and Viṣṇu to reach the head and feet of Śiva, respectively, is alluded to once again.

100

स्तोत्रेणालमहं प्रवच्मि न मृषा देवा विरिञ्चादयः
स्तुत्यानां गणनाप्रसङ्गसमये त्वामग्रगण्यं विदुः ।
माहात्म्याग्रविचारणप्रकरणे धानातुषस्तोमव-
द्धूतास्त्वां विदुरुत्तमोत्तमफलं शंभो भवत्सेवकाः ॥

stotreṇālam ahaṁ pravacmi na mṛṣā devā vīriñcādayaḥ
stutyānāṁ gaṇanāprasaṅgasamaye tvām agragaṇyaṁ viduḥ|
māhātmyāgravicāraṇaprakaraṇe dhānātuṣastomavad-
dhūtās tvāṁ vidur-uttamottamaphalaṁ śambho bhavatsevakāḥ||

O Śaṁbhu! At the time of enumerating those who are worthy of adoration, Thy servants, Brahmā and other gods, know that Thou art the first. While enquiring as to who is the first among the great, they become like chaff covering the grain; they know that Thou art the highest fruit. I am not uttering a falsehood. How am I to praise Thee?

Here, the poem ends, proclaiming Śiva as the supreme Deity. In the assemblage of the gods, He is easily recognized as the foremost God. No praise is adequate to express His greatness. Even to be able to praise Him, His grace is essential.

Plate 4

Śrī Śaṅkara with four disciples (Facing p. 173)

TOṬAKĀṢṬAKAM

A Hymn of Eight Stanzas

By Toṭakācārya

One of the chief disciples of Śaṅkara composed an octad of verses in praise of the Master. The metre he has used in this composition is the difficult but beautiful *toṭaka*. Hence he was himself given the name Toṭakācārya. Every word of this exquisite hymn bespeaks the utter devotion of its author to Śaṅkara. Śaṅkara, the *Guru*, is all to him. There is nothing equal to the *Guru*; nothing superior to Him. The *Guru* is the dispeller of the darkness of ignorance. There can be no greater good than the removal of ignorance. The spirit of devotion of the disciple is best expressed in the soul-moving burden of this song:

Be Thou my refuge, O Master, Śaṅkara (*bhava śaṅkara deśika me śaraṇam*)!

1

विदिताखिलशास्त्रसुधाजलधे महितोपनिषत्कथितार्थनिधे ।
हृदये कलये विमलं चरणं भव शंकर देशिक मे शरणम् ॥

viditākhilaśāstrasudhājaladhe
mahitopaniṣatkathitārthanidhe|
hṛdaye kalaye vimalaṁ caraṇaṁ
bhava śaṅkara deśika me śaraṇam||

O Thou, the knower of all the Milk-Ocean of Scriptures! The expounder of the topics of the great Upaniṣadic treasure-trove! On Thy faultless feet I meditate in my heart, Be Thou my refuge, O Master, Śaṅkara!

2

करुणावरुणालय पालय मां भवसागरदुःखविदूनहृदम् ।
रचयाखिलदर्शनतत्त्वविदं भव शंकर देशिक मे शरणम् ॥

karuṇāvaruṇālaya pālaya māṁ
bhavasāgaraduḥkhavidūnahṛdam|
racayākhiladarśanatattvavidaṁ
bhava śaṅkara deśika me śaraṇam||

O the Ocean of compassion! Save me whose heart is tormented by the misery of the sea of birth! Make me understand the truths of all the schools of philosophy! Be Thou my refuge, O Master, Śaṅkara.

3

भवता जनता सुहिता भविता निजबोधविचारण चारुमते ।
कलयेश्वरजीवविवेकविदं भव शंकर देशिक मे शरणम् ॥३॥

bhavatā janatā suhitā bhavitā
nijabodhavicāraṇa cārumate|
kalayeśvarajīvavivekavidaṁ
bhava śaṅkara deśika me śaraṇam||

By Thee the masses have been made happy, O Thou who hast a noble intellect skilled in the inquiry into self-knowledge! Enable me to understand the wisdom relating to God and the soul. Be Thou my refuge, O Master, Śaṅkara.

4

भव एव भवानिति मे नितरां समजायत चेतसि कौतुकिता ।
मम वारय मोहमहाजलधिं भव शंकर देशिक मे शरणम् ॥

bhava eva bhavāniti me nitarāṁ
samajāyata cetasi kautukitā|
mama vāraya mohamahājaladhiṁ
bhava śaṅkara deśika me śaraṇam||

Knowing that Thou art verily the Supreme Lord, there arises overwhelming bliss in my heart. Protect me from the vast ocean of delusion. Be Thou my refuge, O Master, Śaṅkara.

5

सुकृतेऽधिकृते बहुधा भवतो भविता समदर्शनलालसता ।
अतिदीनमिमं परिपालय मां भव शंकर देशिक मे शरणम् ॥

sukṛte'dhikṛte bahudhā bhavato
bhavitā samadarśanalālasatā|
atidīnamimaṁ paripālaya māṁ
bhava śaṅkara deśika me śaraṇam||

Desire for the insight into unity through Thee will spring only when virtuous deeds are performed in abundance and in various directions. Protect this extremely helpless person. Be Thou my refuge, O Master, Śaṅkara.

6

जगतीमवितुं कलिताकृतयो विचरन्ति महामहसश्छलतः ।
अहिमांशुरिवात्र विभासि गुरो भव शंकर देशिक मे शरणम् ॥

jagatīmavituṁ kalitākṛtayo
vicaranti mahāmahasaśchalataḥ|
ahimāṁśurivātra vibhāsi guro
bhava śaṅkara deśika me śaraṇam||

O Teacher! For saving the world the great assume various forms and wander in disguise.

Of them, Thou shinest like the Sun. Be Thou my refuge, O Master, Śaṅkara.

7

गुरुपुंगव पुंगवकेतन ते समतामयतां नहि कोऽपि सुधीः ।
शरणागतवत्सल तत्त्वनिधे भव शंकर देशिक मे शरणम् ॥

gurupuṅgava puṅgavaketana te
samatāmayatāṁ nahi ko'pi sudhīḥ|
śaraṇāgatavatsala·tattvanidhe
bhava śaṅkara deśika me śaraṇam||

O the best of Teachers! The Supreme Lord having the bull as banner! None of the wise is equal to Thee! Thou who art compassionate to those who have taken refuge ! The Treasure-trove of truth! Be Thou my refuge, O Master Śaṅkara.

8

विदिता न मया विशदैककला न च किंचन काञ्चनमस्ति गुरो ।
द्रुतमेव विधेहि कृपां सहजां भव शंकर देशिक मे शरणम् ॥

viditā na mayā viśadaikakalā
na ca kiṁcana kāñcanamasti guro|
drutameva vidhehi kṛpāṁ sahajāṁ
bhava śaṅkara deśika me śaraṇam||

Not even a single branch of knowledge has been understood by me correctly. Not even the least wealth do I possess, O Teacher. Bestow on me quickly Thy natural grace. Be Thou my refuge, O Master, Śaṅkara.

SELECT VERSES FROM SUREŚVARA'S MĀNASOLLĀSA

1

आत्मलाभात्परो लाभो नास्तीति मुनयो विदुः ।
तल्लाभार्थं कविस्स्तौति स्वात्मानं परमेश्वरम् ॥

ātmalābhāt-paro lābho nāstīti munayo viduḥ|
tal-lābhārthaṁ kavis stauti svātmānam parameśvaram||

That there is no greater gain than the gain of Self, the sages know; for the sake of the gain thereof, the seer-poet (here, Śrī Śaṅkara) sings the praise of the supreme Lord, his own Self.

2

ईश्वरो गुरुरात्मेति मूर्तिभेदविभागिने ।
व्योमवद्व्याप्तदेहाय दक्षिणामूर्तये नमः ॥

īśvaro gurur ātmeti mūrti-bheda-vibhāgine|
vyomavad-vyāpta-dehāya dakṣiṇāmūrtaye namaḥ||

To Him who is differently manifested in the forms of God, the Teacher, and the Self, whose body is all-pervading like ether; to Dakṣiṇāmūrti be this obeisance!

3

सर्वात्मभावना यस्य परिपक्वा महात्मनः ।
संसारतारकस्साक्षात्स एव परमेश्वरः ॥

sarvātmabhāvanā yasya paripakvā mahātmanaḥ|
saṁsāra-tārakassākṣāt sa eva parameśvaraḥ||

The high-souled one whose experience of All-self-hood has become mature is the direct deliverer from *saṁsāra*; he is himself the supreme Lord.

4

अविद्याख्यतिरोधानव्यपाये परमेश्वरः ।
दक्षिणामूर्तिरूपोऽसौ स्वयमेव प्रकाशते ॥

avidyākhya-tirodhāna-vyapāye parameśvaraḥ|
dakṣiṇāmūrtirūpo'sau svayam eva prakāśate||

When the veil which is known as nescience is lifted, the supreme Lord, of the form of Dakṣiṇāmūrti, shines of His own accord.

5

देहेन्द्रियासुहीनाय मानदूरस्वरूपिणे ।
ज्ञानानन्दस्वरूपाय दक्षिणामूर्तये नमः ॥

dehendriyāsu-hīnāya māna-dūra-svarūpiṇe|
jñānānanda-svarūpāya dakṣiṇāmūrtaye namaḥ||

To Him who is without body, sense-organs, and vital airs, whose nature is beyond the means of cognition (perception, etc.), and who is of the nature of consciousness and bliss—to Dakṣiṇāmūrti be this obeisance!

6

निरंशो निर्विकारश्च निराभासो निरञ्जनः ।
पुरुषः केवलः पूर्णः प्रोच्यते परमेश्वरः ॥

niraṁśo nirvikāraśca nirābhāso nirañjanaḥ|
puruṣaḥ kevalaḥ pūrṇaḥ procyate parameśvaraḥ||

The Self is said to be the supreme Lord, who is without parts, without modification, without reflection, pure, alone, and full.

7-8

वाचो यत्र निवर्तन्ते मनो यत्र विलीयते ।
एकीभवन्ति यत्रैव भूतानि भुवनानि च ॥
समस्तानि च तत्त्वानि समुद्रे सिन्धवो यथा ।
कश्शोकस्तत्र को मोह एकत्वमनुपश्यतः ॥

vāco yatra nivartante mano yatra vilīyate|
ekībhavanti yatraiva bhūtāni bhuvanāni ca||
samastāni ca tattvāni samudre sindhavo yathā|
kaśśokastatra ko moha ekatvam-anupaśyataḥ||

That wherefrom words return and wherein the mind is resolved, that wherewith beings and worlds become one, and all the principles too, like the rivers with the ocean—what sorrow is there, what delusion, to the one who sees the one-ness?

9

सच्चिदानन्दरूपाय बिन्दुनादान्तरात्मने ।
आदिमध्यान्तशून्याय गुरूणां गुरवे नमः ॥

saccidānanda-rūpāya bindunādāntarātmane|
ādimadhyāntaśūnyāya gurūṇāṁ gurave namaḥ||

To the preceptor of preceptors, who is of the form of the existence-consciousness-bliss, who is the inner self of *bindu* and *nāda*, who is without beginning, middle and end, be this obeisance!

10

स्तोत्रमेतत्पठेद्धीमान् सर्वात्मत्वं च भावयेत् ।
अर्वाचीने स्पृहां मुक्त्वा फले स्वर्गादिसम्भवे ॥

stotram etat paṭhed dhīmān sarvātmatvaṁ ca bhāvayet|
arvācīne spṛhāṁ muktvā phale svargādi-sambhave||

Let the wise one read this hymn and contemplate All-Self-hood, leaving all yearning for the smaller fruit arising out of heaven, etc.

11

स्वर्गादिराज्यं साम्राज्यं मनुते न हि पण्डितः ।
तदेव तस्य साम्राज्यं यत्तु स्वाराज्यमात्मनि ॥

svargādi-rājyaṁ sāmrājyaṁ manute na hi paṇḍitaḥ|
tad eva tasya sāmrājyaṁ yat tu svārājyam ātmani||

The wise one does not deem the sovereignty of heaven, etc., as universal empery; that alone is universal empery for him, which is autonomy with reference to the Self.

12

सर्वात्मभावनावन्तं सेवन्ते सर्वसिद्धयः ।
तस्मादात्मनि साम्राज्यं कुर्यान्नियतमानसः ॥

sarvātmabhāvanāvantaṁ sevante sarva-siddhayaḥ|
tasmād ātmani sāmrājyaṁ kuryān niyata-mānasaḥ||

All supernormal powers serve him who has the experience of All-Self-hood. Therefore, let one exercise universal empery in regard to the Self, having controlled his mind.

13

यस्य देवे परा भक्तिर्यथा देवे तथा गुरौ ।
तस्यैते कथिता ह्यर्थाः प्रकाशन्ते महात्मनः ।।

yasya deve parā bhaktir yathā deve tathā gurau|
tasyaite kathitā hyarthāḥ prakāśante mahātmanaḥ||

To that high-souled one, who has supreme devotion for God, and for the preceptor as for God, shine in full the truths that are taught here.

14

प्रकाशात्मिकया शक्त्या प्रकाशानां प्रभाकरः ।
प्रकाशयति यो विश्वं प्रकाशोऽयं प्रकाशताम् ।।

prakāśātmikayā śaktyā prakāśānāṁ prabhākaraḥ|
prakāśayati yo viśvaṁ prakāśoyaṁ prakāśatām||

That Luminosity which illumines all luminaries by its power of luminosity, that which illumines the universe—may that shine in full!

GLOSSARY

Ācārya:	Preceptor
Ādi:	Beginning; origin; first one
Adikutumba:	First family (Śiva-Pārvatī)
Advaita:	Non-duality
Ajaḍa:	Non-inert
Ajñāna:	Ignorance
Alaṅkāra:	Adornment
Amanībhāva:	Mindlessness
Amṛta:	Ambrosia
Amūrta:	Without form
Ānanda:	Bliss
Anirvacanīya:	Indeterminable
Aṅkola:	A kind of tree
Anugraha:	Bestowal of grace
Apasmāra:	The dwarf representing nescience whereon the foot of Śiva as Dakṣiṇāmūrti and Naṭarāja etc., is placed
Ārambhaka:	Originating cause
Ardhanārīśvara:	Half-male half-female form of Śiva
Arcana:	Offering worship
Asat:	Non-existence
Asatkārya-vāda:	The view which says that the effect is non-existent in the cause
Āśraya:	Locus
Aṣṭamūrta:	Eightfold form of Śiva
Ātman:	Self
Ātmanivedana:	Self-gift to God
Ātmavañcaka:	Deceiver of Self
Avidyā	Nescience
Avyākulacitta:	Untroubled mind
Bālonmattapiśācavat:	Like a child, lunatic and ghost
Bhāga-tyāga-lakṣaṇā	Exclusive-non-exclusive implication, Jahad-ajahal-lakṣaṇā
Bhaja:	Adore, serve, worship

Bhakti:	Devotion
Bhikṣu:	Mendicant
Bhūman:	Infinite
Bindu:	Central point
Bodha:	Knowledge
Brahman:	The absolute Self
Buddhi:	Intellect
Cakora:	Bird which is sustained by lunar rays
Cakravāka:	Bird which looks forward to sunrise
Candra:	Moon
Cārvāka or Lokāyata:	Materialism
Caryā:	This is the first step in Śaiva discipline: cleaning temples etc.
Cātaka:	Bird which drinks rain-drops from the clouds
Cetas:	Consciousness
Cidālambam:	The basis of consciousness
Cidānandam:	Consciousness-bliss
Cinmudrā:	Symbol of pure consciousness indicated by the thumb and fore-finger of the right hand touching together
Cintāmaṇi:	Wishfulfilling jewel
Cit:	Consciousness
Citta:	Mind
Dakṣiṇaḥ:	One who is expert in accomplishing (origination, sustenance and destruction of the world).
Dāsya:	Servitude
Deva:	Deity
Dharma:	Virtue
Dhī:	Wisdom
Dhṛti:	Resolve, strength of will
Dhyāna-śloka:	Meditation-verse
Dīna-bandhuḥ:	Friend of the poor
Dīna-rakṣakaḥ:	Protector of the poor
Dṛṣṭānta:	Example
Ḍukṛñ karaṇe:	Sūtra from Pāṇini's grammar
Durgā:	Name of Goddess

Guṇa:	Constituent of Prakṛti; attribute or qualification
Gaurīpatiḥ:	Lord of Gauri
Guru:	Teacher
Halāhala:	Poison which came out of the churning of the ocean
Haṁsa:	Swan; saint; sage
Hetu:	Reason; ground; *probans*
Hetūpanaya:	Application of *probans*
Hṛdaya:	Heart; emotional side of mind
Ikṣuraka:	Flower without fragrance or honey
Iṣṭa:	Chosen deity
Īśvara:	God
Īśvaratva:	Lordship
Jaḍa:	Inert
Jagadadhika:	Exceeding the world
Jaṭābhāra:	One with matted locks
Jīva:	Individual soul
Jīvanmukta:	One liberated while living
Jīvatva:	Soulhood
Kalā:	Part
Kalpavṛkṣa:	Wishfulfilling-tree
Kāmadhenu:	The heavenly cow of plenty
Kapāli:	He who bears the scull for alms-bowl
Kāraṇa:	Cause
Karma:	Action; result of action
Kīrtana:	Singing praise of God
Kriyā:	Second step in Śaiva discipline: offering formal worship
Kṣaṇikavijñāna:	Momentary cognition
Kaṭhina:	Hard to remove
Liṅga:	A Symbol; the sign of Śiva
Lokaguru:	World teacher
Mahādeva:	Great God (Śiva)
Mahāvākya:	Major text
Manana:	Reflection
Manas:	Mind

Maṅgalācaraṇa:	Paying obeisance to God or Guru at the beginning of a work, as a sign of auspiciousness
Mantra:	Sacred syllable
Māyā:	Illusion
Mithyācāra:	Hypocrite
Mokṣa:	Release; liberation
Mūḍhamatiḥ:	Fool
Nāda:	Sound
Nididhyāsana:	Meditation
Nigamana:	Conclusion in an inference
Nīlagrīva:	Blue-throated one (Śiva)
Nīlakaṇṭha:	Blue-throated one (Śiva)
Nindāstuti:	Praise disguised as blame
Niravayava:	Partless
Niṣprapañca:	Void of the universe
Nyāya Vaiśeṣika:	Logical Realism and Atomism (Two allied systems of philosophy)
Pādasevana:	Adoring the feet of the Lord
Parameśvara:	The supreme Lord
Pariṇāma:	Transformation
Pañcamukha:	One with five faces; a lion; Śiva
Phalaśruti:	A statement of the fruit (of any recitation etc.)
Pradhāna:	Primal nature
Prakṛti:	Primal nature (same as Pradhāna)
Prāṇa:	Vital principle
Pratijñā:	A statement; a declaration
Pratipakṣabhāvanā:	Thinking the opposite
Preyas:	Pleasure
Puṇyāha:	Rite performed for purifying a place
Puṇyāhavācana:	Ritual for purification
Purahāra:	He who destroyed the three cities
Puruṣa:	Sentient soul
Rasa:	Aesthetic enjoyment
Sādhusamāgama:	Company of the good
Saguṇa:	With qualities
Sakhya:	Friendship

Sākṣātkāra:	Direct experience
Sālokya:	Sameness of residence
Sama:	Sameness
Śama:	Calmness
Samacitta:	Sameness of mind
Śambhu:	Source of auspiciousness; name of Śiva
Saṁhāra:	Destruction
Sāmīpya:	Nearness to God
Saṁsāra:	Transmigration
Śaṅkara:	One who does what is auspicious; a name of Śiva, Śaṅkarācārya
Sāṅkhya:	One of the systems of philosophy which believes in two categories: spirit and primal matter
Sannyāsin:	Renunciate
Santoṣa:	Contentment
Sārūpya:	Sameness of form
Sarvātmatva:	All-Selfhood
Śāstra:	Scripture
Sat:	Real
Sattva:	Purity (one of the three guṇas)
Sāyujya:	Union
Śeṣa:	Surplus; what remains; what is auxiliary
Siddha:	One who is accomplished in yoga
Śiṣṭāgraṇīḥ:	The foremost among the cultured
Śiṣya:	Disciples
Śiva:	One who is auspicious
Śleṣa:	Employing words in a double sense
Smaraṇa:	Thinking of God
Soma:	Purifying a place; sacred point; moon
Śravaṇa:	Listening
Śreyas:	Good
Sṛṣṭi:	Creation
Sthāṇu:	The stable one; the unshakeable one; (Śiva)

Sthitaprajña:	Steadfast in wisdom
Sthiti:	Preservation
Sthūla:	Gross
Stotra:	Hymn
Sūkṣma:	Subtle
Sūtra:	Aphorism
Svabhāvavāda:	Naturalism
Svarūpānusandhānalakṣaṇam:	Characterized by remembering the Self
Tamas:	(literally darkness); one of the three guṇas
Tamassukha;	Pleasure of the lowest type
Tapasyā:	Austerity
Tattvas:	Principles
Tirodhāna:	Veiling
Toṭaka:	A metre
Trinayana:	With three eyes
Tripurahāra:	He who destroyed the three cities
Tripurāri:	The enemy of the three cities
Uparama:	Quiescence
Vāda:	View, Disputation
Vairāgya:	Dispassion
Vandana:	Making obeisance
Vāsanā:	Tendency, residual impression
Vedānta:	End (goal) of the Veda
Vicāra:	Enquiry
Vilāsa:	Play
Viṣaya:	Content
Viśvādhika:	More than the world
Viśva-māyā:	All-māyā
Viśveśa:	Lord of the world
Vitṛṣṇa:	Non-thirst
Vivarta:	Illusory appearance
Vyākulacitta:	Troubled mind
Yadṛcchāvāda:	Accidentalism
Yogācāra:	Subjective Idealism (one of the schools of Buddhism)
Yogin:	Expert in yoga